First World War
and Army of Occupation
War Diary
France, Belgium and Germany

18 DIVISION
Headquarters, Branches and Services
Commander Royal Engineers
25 July 1915 - 1 April 1919

WO95/2023/1

The Naval & Military Press Ltd
www.nmarchive.com
Published in association with The National Archives

Published by

The Naval & Military Press Ltd

Unit 10 Ridgewood Industrial Park,

Uckfield, East Sussex,

TN22 5QE England

Tel: +44 (0) 1825 749494

www.naval-military-press.com

www.nmarchive.com

This diary has been reprinted in facsimile from the original. Any imperfections are inevitably reproduced and the quality may fall short of modern type and cartographic standards.

© Crown Copyright
Images reproduced by permission of The National Archives, London, England, 2015.

Contents

Document type	Place/Title	Date From	Date To
Heading	WO95/2023/1		
Heading	18th Division C. R.E. Jly 1915-Apl 1919		
Heading	H.Q. 18th Division CRE. Vol I July to October 15		
War Diary	Southampton	25/07/1915	25/07/1915
War Diary	Le Havre	26/07/1915	27/07/1915
War Diary	Longeau	28/07/1915	28/07/1915
War Diary	Flesselles	28/07/1915	08/08/1915
War Diary	St Gratien	08/08/1915	19/08/1915
War Diary	Heilly	19/08/1915	15/10/1915
Heading	H.Q. 18th Div: CRE. Vol 2 121/7624 Nov 15		
War Diary		00/11/1915	00/11/1915
Miscellaneous	Blocks of Buildings Completed Or Under Construction.		
Heading	CRE. 18th Div: Vol: 3 121/7935		
War Diary		00/12/1915	00/12/1915
Miscellaneous	List of Changes In Officers. R.E 18th Division.		
Heading	CRE. 18th Div. Vol. 4 Jan		
War Diary	Heilly	01/01/1916	31/01/1916
Heading	C.R.E. 18th Div Vol. 5		
War Diary	Ribemont	01/02/1916	29/02/1916
War Diary	In The Field	06/03/1916	21/03/1916
War Diary	In Field	01/04/1916	30/04/1916
War Diary	In The Field	01/05/1916	31/05/1916
Heading	War Diary of R.E. H.Q. 18 Div. Period April to June 1916		
War Diary			
War Diary	Chipilly	21/06/1916	21/06/1916
War Diary		19/06/1916	19/06/1916
War Diary	B.H.Q.	24/06/1916	26/06/1916
Operation(al) Order(s)	? Operation Order No 1	28/06/1916	28/06/1916
Heading	C.R E July 16 Vol 10 18 Div		
War Diary		01/07/1916	31/07/1916
War Diary	Croix Du Bac	01/08/1916	24/08/1916
War Diary	Bailleul	25/08/1916	25/08/1916
War Diary	Boiran	26/08/1916	08/09/1916
War Diary	Doullens	09/09/1916	09/09/1916
War Diary	Acheux	11/09/1916	23/09/1916
War Diary	Hedauville	25/09/1916	30/09/1916
War Diary		07/09/1916	23/09/1916
War Diary	Hedauville	01/10/1916	05/10/1916
War Diary	Bernaville 'Q' Area	06/10/1916	15/10/1916
War Diary	Albert	16/10/1916	21/10/1916
War Diary	Tara Hill	22/10/1916	31/10/1916
War Diary	H.Q. Tara Hill Albert.	01/11/1916	01/12/1916
War Diary	Chateau Ouville	08/12/1916	31/12/1916
War Diary		22/12/1916	22/12/1916
War Diary	Ouville	01/01/1917	12/01/1917
War Diary	Bernaville	13/01/1917	14/01/1917
War Diary	Marieux	15/01/1917	15/01/1917
War Diary	Bouzincourt	16/01/1917	31/01/1917

Type	Description	Date From	Date To
Miscellaneous	Operation Orders by Lieut Colonel H. M. Henderson R.E., C.R.E., 18th Division Headquarters. R.E. 18th Division.	16/02/1917	16/02/1917
Miscellaneous	Orders by Lieut Colonel H.M. Henderson R.E., C.R.E., 18th Division Headquarters R.E., 18th Division.	20/02/1917	20/02/1917
Miscellaneous			
Miscellaneous	Operation Orders by Lieut Colonel H. M. Henderson R.E., Commanding Royal Engineer, 18th Division. Headquarters. R.E., 18th Division.	08/03/1917	08/03/1917
Miscellaneous			
War Diary	Bois lens St Marc	09/06/1917	09/06/1917
War Diary	Renninghelst	08/06/1917	08/06/1917
War Diary	Dickebusch	06/08/1917	06/08/1917
Miscellaneous	Instructions To Royal Engineers For Forthcoming Operations	17/07/1917	17/07/1917
Miscellaneous	Distribution:-		
Miscellaneous	Instructions For The 8th Royal Sussex Pioneers And The Battalion of The 55th Brigade Allotted To C.R.E. For Work On Z Day	17/07/1917	17/07/1917
Miscellaneous	Disposition of R.E. And Pioneer Units On "Z" Day		
War Diary	Esquelbec	23/09/1917	23/09/1917
War Diary	Poperinghe	24/09/1917	29/09/1917
War Diary	Elverdinghe	10/10/1917	10/10/1917
Heading	Headquarters. 18th Division. A. Herewith War Diaries for the 18th Divisional Engineers for the Month of November 1917		
War Diary	Elverdinghe	09/11/1917	01/01/1918
War Diary	Rouez	01/02/1918	01/02/1918
Operation(al) Order(s)	18th Division. C. R.E.'s Operation Order. No. 25.	23/02/1918	23/02/1918
Heading	War Diary Headquarters, Royal Engineers, 18th Division. March 1918		
War Diary	Rouez	01/03/1918	01/03/1918
War Diary	St-Quentin Sheet	01/03/1918	01/03/1918
Operation(al) Order(s)	18th Division. C.R.E's Operation Order. No. 26.	09/03/1918	09/03/1918
Heading	Headquarters, Royal Engineers, 18th Division. April 1918		
War Diary	Cavillon Ref Amiens Sheet 1/100.000	01/04/1918	01/04/1918
War Diary			
War Diary	Contay. Sheet. 57/D.	09/06/1918	09/06/1918
Miscellaneous	Nominal Roll of Officers. 18th Divisional Engineers.	29/06/1918	29/06/1918
Operation(al) Order(s)	18th Division. C. R.E.'s Operation Order No. 131.	12/06/1918	12/06/1918
Operation(al) Order(s)	18th Division. C. R.E.'s Operation Order No. 132.	26/06/1918	26/06/1918
Miscellaneous	War Diary. Reference my order No. 132 (attached)	26/06/1918	26/06/1918
War Diary	St. Gratien. Sheet. 62.D.	10/08/1918	10/08/1918
Miscellaneous	Nominal Roll of Officers.-18th Divisional Engineers.		
Miscellaneous	Casualties And Changes During The Month of July.		
Operation(al) Order(s)	18th Division. C. R.E.'s Operation Order. No. 133.	28/07/1918	28/07/1918
Miscellaneous	Move Table to Accompany C.R.E.'s. Order No. 133.		
Heading	18th Division. C. R.E. 18th Division August 1918		
War Diary	St. Gratien. Sheet 62.D.	01/08/1918	11/08/1918
War Diary	Contay. Sheet 57.D.	12/08/1918	22/08/1918
War Diary	Henencourt Sheet 57.D.	24/08/1918	31/08/1918
Miscellaneous	Appendices Attached.		
Miscellaneous	Nominal Roll of Officers.-18th Divisional Engineers.		
Miscellaneous	Casualties And Changes During The Month of August.		
Operation(al) Order(s)	18th Division. C.R.E.'s. Operation Order. No. 136.	20/08/1918	20/08/1918

Type	Description	From	To
Heading	Headquarters 18th Divl. Engineers. Appendix to War Diary for August.		
War Diary	Montauban	01/08/1918	02/08/1918
War Diary	Combles	03/08/1918	04/08/1918
War Diary	Montauban	05/08/1918	16/08/1918
War Diary	Lieramont.	17/08/1918	24/08/1918
War Diary	Combles.	25/08/1918	27/08/1918
War Diary	Lieramont.	28/08/1918	30/08/1918
Miscellaneous	List of Documents attached to War Diary for September 1918	11/10/1918	11/10/1918
Operation(al) Order(s)	18th Division. C.R.E.'s. Operation Order. No. 137.	15/09/1918	15/09/1918
Miscellaneous	O.C. 79th Field Coy. R.E. O.C. 80th Field Coy. R.E. O.C. 92nd Field Coy. R.E.	15/09/1918	15/09/1918
Miscellaneous	Provisional Bus Arrangements Table "A"		
Operation(al) Order(s)	18th Division. C.R.E.'s. Operation Order. No. 138.	24/09/1918	24/09/1918
Operation(al) Order(s)	18th Division. C.R.E.'s Operation Order. No. 139.	27/09/1918	27/09/1918
Miscellaneous	Field Company Commanders. O.C. 8th R. Sussex Regt.		
Miscellaneous	Nominal Roll of Officers.-18th Divisional Engineers.		
Miscellaneous	Casualties And Changes During The Month of September.	01/10/1918	01/10/1918
Heading	Headquarters, 18th Division. Herewith War Diary for H.Q. R.E. 18th Division, and Diaries for 79th. 80th. 92nd Field Coys R.E. for the Month of October 1918		
War Diary	Lieramont.	01/10/1918	01/10/1918
War Diary	Beaucourt	02/10/1918	17/10/1918
War Diary	Ronssoy Wood	18/10/1918	19/10/1918
War Diary	Serain	20/10/1918	20/10/1918
War Diary	Maretz	21/10/1918	23/10/1918
War Diary	Le Cateau.	24/10/1918	31/10/1918
Operation(al) Order(s)	18th Division Order No. 235. C.R.E.'s. Instructions No. 1.	20/10/1918	20/10/1918
Miscellaneous	Nominal Roll of Officers.-18th Divisional Engineers.		
Miscellaneous	Casualties And Changes During The Month of October.	01/11/1918	01/11/1918
War Diary	Le Cateau.	01/11/1918	06/11/1918
War Diary	Noyelles	13/11/1918	18/11/1918
War Diary	Maurois.	19/11/1918	19/11/1918
War Diary	Serain.	19/11/1918	30/11/1918
Miscellaneous	Distribution.		
Miscellaneous	18th Division. C.R.E.'s Instructions No. 1.	01/11/1918	01/11/1918
Miscellaneous	18th Division. C.R.E.'s Instructions No. 2.	03/11/1918	03/11/1918
Miscellaneous	Nominal Roll of Officers.-18th Divisional Engineers.		
Miscellaneous	Casualties And Changes During the Month.	30/11/1918	30/11/1918
War Diary	Serain.	01/12/1918	31/12/1918
Miscellaneous	Nominal Roll of Officers.-18th Divisional Engineers.	01/12/1918	01/12/1918
Miscellaneous	Casualties And Changes During The Month of December	01/01/1919	01/01/1919
War Diary	Ligny.	01/01/1919	31/01/1919
War Diary	Ligny-En Cambresis. (Nord.)	01/02/1919	28/02/1919
Miscellaneous	Nominal Roll of Officers.-18th Divisional Engineers.		
Miscellaneous	Casualties And Changes During February. 1919	28/02/1919	28/02/1919
Heading	18th Division 'A'.		
War Diary	Ligny-En-Cambresis (Nord.)	01/03/1919	31/03/1919
Miscellaneous	Nominal Roll of Officers.-18th Divisional Engineers.		
Miscellaneous	Casualties And Changes During The Month of March 1919 79th Field Company R.E.	28/03/1919	28/03/1919
Heading	Headquarters. 18th Division Packet.		

War Diary   Ligny-En-Cambresis. (Nord.)   01/04/1919   31/04/1919

WP 96/2023(1)

18TH DIVISION

C. R. E.

JLY 1915 - APL 1919

18TH DIVISION

121/7517

H.Q. 8th Division CRE.
Vol I
July to October 15

Apl 19

Army Form C. 2118

WAR DIARY
of C.R.E. 13th Div.
INTELLIGENCE SUMMARY
(Erase heading not required.)

July 1915

Original

Place	Date	Hour	Summary of Events and Information	Remarks and references to Appendices
Southampton	25/7/15	4 PM	The Headquarters, 13th Div. Engineers embarked. Strength:- CRE (Lt Col C. Skinner R.E.) Adjutant. Medical Officer. O.R. 9 attached O.R. 2 (ASC) Horses 7, attached 4 (ASC).	3
Le Havre	26/7/15	10 AM	Disembarked and proceeded to Rest Camp	
do	27/7/15	2 PM	entrained.	
Longeau	28/7/15	3 AM	detrained	
Flesselles	28/7/15	10 AM	arrived.	
	29/7/15		80th Fd Coy R.E. arrived TALMAS	
	30/7/15		79th Fd Coy R.E. arrived SEPTONVILLE	
	31/7/15		92nd Fd Coy R.E. arrived COISY	

A.S....
Capt M.E.
Adjt 13th Div R.E.
31-7-15

Army Form C. 2118

WAR DIARY
of CRE 18th Division
INTELLIGENCE SUMMARY
(Erase heading not required.)

August 1914

August 1915 ①

Place	Date	Hour	Summary of Events and Information	Remarks and references to Appendices
FLESSELLES	1/8/15 to 7/8/15		At FLESSELLES with Divisional Headquarters. The Division was concentrating during this time. The CRE took advantage of this pause to install At Leinster with the chief Engineers and with the Divisional Commander. A section of the 80th Coy RE were employed at Divisional Headquarters for some days in wood cutting and other work. The 79th Coy went for instruction to ANELUY to work under 51st Divn. The 80th and 92nd Coy went to SENLIS and MILLENCOURT respectively to work on the 2nd line under the Chief Engineer X Corps.	
FLESSELLES	8/8/15	9PM	HQ RE moved to ST GRATIEN	
ST GRATIEN	do	5 PM	" arrived at "	
			The 79th Coy now went to BRAY, and the 80th Coy to MEAULTE do work on C and D sectors respectively, the 92nd Coy remains under the CE X Corps at MILLENCOURT	
ST GRATIEN	19.8.14	2 PM	moved to HEILLY	
HEILLY	do	4.30 PM	arrived Divl HQ HEILLY. The Division now proceeded to take over C and D sectors	4

WAR DIARY of CRE 18th Divn
INTELLIGENCE SUMMARY

Army Form C. 2118

August 1915

Place	Date	Hour	Summary of Events and Information	Remarks and references to Appendices
HEILLY	19-8-15 to 31-8-15		The trenches were visited several times by the CRE, and schemes for water supply to the trenches, dread Tramways, etc were worked out. A conference at RAINCHEVAL at Chief Engineer and CRE's was attended by the CRE 19.8.15. 6 proposals for road maintenance, supplies of stores, etc were made. Wood cutting was undertaken at BEAUCOURT by a company of the Sussex Pioneers and a good deal of timber, brushwood etc was supplied to the 79th Coy at BRAY. The 79th Coy started making dugouts for a reserve battalion about 1½ miles N E of BRAY. Casualty Officer Lieut Alan Wilson 79th Fd Coy R.E. died on 25.8.15	5

Morrall
Major RE
Adjt 18th Dn R.E.
31.8.15

WAR DIARY of CRE 18th Divr.

INTELLIGENCE SUMMARY

Sept 1915

Place	Date	Hour	Summary of Events and Information	Remarks and references to Appendices
HEILLY	1/9/15		Lt Col C Shinner R.E. having been placed on special duty under C.E. X Corps, Major H.G. Joly de Lotbinière D.S.O R.E. took over the duties of CRE 18th Divn. The R.E. were employed as follows: 79th Field Coy was at BRAY. Attached to 53rd Inf Bde and was working in C¹ and C² sectors: the 80th Field Coy was stationed at MEAULTE and was employed on D¹ - D² - D³ sectors with the 54th and 55th Bdes. The 92nd Fld Coy remained under the X Corps at MILLENCOURT.	
	15/9/15		The 18th Division started going over C¹, A¹, C² sectors to the 51st Divn. and took over E¹, E², E³ sectors from the 51st Divn. The 79th Fd Coy was transferred to ALBERT with the 53rd Bde, and shortly afterwards the 92nd Fd Coy (less one section) was attached to the 55th Inf Bde being stationed at BERNANCOURT. The duties of the R.E. sections gunnison was now: 80th Coy Att. 54th Bde working in D¹, D² sector. 55th " 53rd " 92nd " 79th " D³, E¹ " E², E³ "	6

WAR DIARY
or INTELLIGENCE SUMMARY

Army Form C. 2118

Sept 1915 (2)

5 RB 12th Div

Sept 1915 page 2

During the month the CRE's lines were taken up with

(1) The formation of R.E. Parks at Dernancourt and Buray.
The Parks being transferred on 15.9.15 to ALBERT

(2) The organization for cutting lumber from local sources
   BOIS DES TAILLES — Birch, hornbeam, brushwood, &c
   VILLE SUR ANCRE — Poplar, Ander

(3) Laying out new communication trenches and the front occupied by the Div:

(4) Water supply to D.3 Subsector.

(5) Starting a circular saw at DERNANCOURT

(6) Survey of the ground in connection with the Battalion Redoubt, and the I Termediate Line

(7) Supervising installation of Baths and Laundries at Ville s/Ancre and HEILLY
      Rest Station, DAOURS
   "   Canteen and Recreation Room at MERICOURT
   "

(10) Appreciation of progress received attention.

(11) Allotments of work to the Pioneers.

WAR DIARY
of CRE 18th Div.
INTELLIGENCE SUMMARY

Army Form C. 2118

Sept 1915 (3)

Sept 1915 page 3

(11) Preparation of D' sector for an advance : special bombproofs were constructed, ALBERT and MARTYN Avenues were prepared as forming up places. These trenches were heavily traversed and revetted.

(13) The 122nd Fd Coy R.E. and the Pioneer Regt of the 22nd Divn were attached for one week under instruction and were chiefly employed in D' sector preparing for the advance alluded to in (11).

Changes in staff during month –

HQ
Fd Scott RAMC with medical orderly and batman proceeded from Div HQ HEILLY to MEAULTE to be stationed there.

79th Coy
2nd Lt E P Stevenson joined 12.9.15
                          wounded 20.9.15
2nd Lt J F Wilson joined 28.9.15

80th Coy
Capt F J M King assumed command 1.9.15
2 Lt H C C WALKEM joined 7.9.15

8

Nov Batter
Maj C in Dr CE
Ack 1915 –
3 Oct 15 –

WAR DIARY or INTELLIGENCE SUMMARY

Army Form C. 2118

of CRE 18th Divn October 1915

Place	Date	Hour	Summary of Events and Information	Remarks and references to Appendices
HEILLY	2/10/15	—	Capt. Grant R.E. rejoined the H.Q. 18th Divn R.E. for special duty in connection with under accommodation.	
	15/10/15	—	The last section of 92nd Coy R.E. rejoined the division from employment under 8th X Corps. The work done by the 18th Divl. R.E. during October may be summarised as under:—	

NEW TRENCHES

The 79th Coy constructed   PAGET ST (50')
                           KIRRIEMUIR ST (100')
                           KINFAUNS ST (300')
                           Evacuation trench from
                           ARBROATH ST to SCOURING BURN ST
                           (60' 2' 0" finished)

80th Coy. constructed and remodelled MAPLE REDOUBT (O.1)
                                      BECORDEL defences.

92nd Coy converted communication trench from
BON ACCORD & MARISCHAL ST
into fire trench

completed communication trench from
ALBERT to BECOURT

9

Army Form C. 2118

WAR DIARY of CRE 18th Divn
INTELLIGENCE SUMMARY

October 1915 (contd)

October 1915

2. **Old Trenches**: a large number were repaired, strengthened and deepened.

3. **New Bombproofs**

79th Coy constructed Aid Post in PANMURE ST. Splinter proof R: too post N° 114, reserve for 250 men in S:ANDREWS AV and KINFAUNS ST. Shellproofs for 2 – ½ platoons.

86th Coy completed 7 and started 18 more.

92nd Coy " 6 " 5 "

4. **Water Supply** (d) 800ˣ men load from ALBERT towards LA BOISELLE.
(e) Water supply to D₂, D₃, and E, practically completed.

5. Buildings and accessories for troops out of the trenches.

The question of improving billets received considerable attention.

10

WAR DIARY of 2nd/18th Div
INTELLIGENCE SUMMARY October 1915

(2)

Many of the billets were fitted up as Company or Platoon dining room, cookhouse, ablution places and drying rooms were fitted up. Whenever possible these were adapted from existing buildings; in a few cases only were new buildings found necessary.

The provision of benches, tables and other fittings proceeded rapidly.

6. Horse standings. All mounted units practically completed their horse standings which were of rough schemes from ruined houses in ALBERT. The question of watering arrangements and overhead cover for horses commenced to receive attention.

7. Wood cutting. No 16 Platoon R.S. Pioneers was detailed for wood cutting, which was done in

HEILLY – Poplar.
BUIRE – do.
ST GRATIEN – Brushwood and pickets.
RIBEMONT & LAHOUSSOYE – 6" to 10" beech trees.

8. 91 Sub.Cy. R.E. Abt. About 500 tons of wood in are cut and despatches to the trenches.

11

WAR DIARY
INTELLIGENCE SUMMARY

of CRE 18th Divn.
October 1915

Army Form C. 2118

4

12

8 Supply of Trenches. 6 motor lorries were employed in carrying branch Avre from the R.S. Peut at ACHEUX to the R.E. Parks at DERNANCOURT and ALBERT. On the 28th October the R.S. Park at MERICOURT (No 1) was closed for the X Corps. About 300 tons of trench stores were taken up during the month at MERICOURT & were recalled on 28.10.15 for employment on Railways Lid. They were recalled on 31.10.15.

9 The 107th Coy R.E. from the 26th (R.D.)
10 Circular Saws were installed at ALBERT (Av), DERNANCOURT (by the 97th Fd Coy) and at TREUX.

11 Drainage of trenches continued to receive attention. 1400' of trench will was laid (South Avenue 1st Dn and E)

Ashley
Major
A.D. 18th Divn R.E.
31.10.15

13

HQ. 18th Div:
CRE.
vol: 2

121/7624

Nov 15

SECRET

Army Form C. 2118

WAR DIARY of the 18th Bns.

INTELLIGENCE SUMMARY Nov. 1915.

(Erase heading not required.)

Place	Date	Hour	Summary of Events and Information	Remarks and references to Appendices
Nov 1915			The work of the R.E. 18th Bns. during Nov. may be summarised as follows:-	
			(a) <u>Firing trenches.</u> Boards walk laid in	
			D₁ sector — Back Lane, WITHAN St, 70 St	
			D₂ sector — From Small Avenue to D.2 H.Q	
			D₃ sector — (a). Continued in King's Avenue.	
			(b). From Tambour to new sandbag dump.	
			E₁ sector — Continued in Aberdeen Avenue.	
			E₂ } sectors — about 2,400 yds laid of board grating	
			E₃ }	
			several used for bunching up and low lying places.	
			(b) <u>Dumps.</u> —	
			(c) <u>Communications.</u> — a new sandbag dump constructed close to TAMBOUR; new communication trench cut and provided with trolley track of TAMBOUR revetted & facilitate traffic.	
			(d) <u>Shelters</u> — several completed in D₁, D₂, D₃, & E₁ sectors.	
			10 dugouts, deep mined huts in hand in E₂ & E₃ sectors (5 completed)	1F

WAR DIARY
of CRE 18th
INTELLIGENCE SUMMARY Nov: 1915

(Erase heading not required.)

Army Form C. 2118

Place	Date	Hour	Summary of Events and Information	Remarks and references to Appendices

(e) Lighting and Heating Stoves and lamps started coming in and have been installed in dining and recreation rooms.

(f) Bath Stoves E. One bath stove completed.

Recesses in the trenches are being lined & kept out rain and damp.

(g) Tramways
(1) One constructed between the Citadel and D, HQ.
(2) One from BARAUME POST to new cookhouses.
(3) E₃ approved but not yet commenced.

(h) General
Water supply completed to D₂, HQ, Bode, R 3 and E.1.
Pipe extended from D.3. HQ to D.3. Cookers and water laid on. Pipe extended from E Cookers to E.1. HQ and water laid on to large tank. Water supply for the supply of E 3 and new cookhouses as well as NINA and TURA redoubts almost completed.

SECRET

Army Form C. 2118

WAR DIARY
CRA 13th Div
INTELLIGENCE SUMMARY Nov 1915
(Erase heading not required.)

3

16

Summary of Events and Information

Winter Accommodation. Considerable progress has been made in hutted accommodation in billets during the month.

Blocks of buildings in accordance with the attached table have been completed or are under construction. Each block consists of a company dining room, cookhouse, drying room, ablution room, and latrines.

Horse shelter. Mounted units have completed their standings, some form of shelter, and suitable watering arrangements have been provided.

Wood cutting. No 16 Recn R.S. Pioneers continued to cut wood in HEILLY, BONNAY, BUIRE, *VILLE, ST GRATIEN (hopehus) and brushwood at ST GRATIEN. About 160 tons of wood were despatched to the saw mills or trenches.

30-11-15

[signature]
Maj RE
A/CRE 13th Div RE

Blocks of Buildings completed or under construction.

-o-o-o-o-o-o-o-o-o-o-o-

Place.	Completed.	Nearly completed.	Under construction.	Remarks.
BUIRE.	1	3	1	
VILLE-SUR-ANCRE.	4 (a)	2		(a) one block not furnished.
MERICOURT.	3		2	
TREUX.	4			
RIPEMONT.	1	3		
BONNAY.		4		
DAOURS.				Rest Station completed.
HEILLY.	5	3		
MOULIN-DU-VIVIER.	1	2		
MORLANCOURT.				Several accessory buildings completed.

AT ALBERT   Dining rooms for all infantry Coys completed. Stoves are now being put in.

AT MEAULTE. The work is in hand and will be completed during the next fortnight.

CRF. 18e sér.
vol. 3

121/1935

18

WAR DIARY
of C.R.E. 13th Div.
INTELLIGENCE SUMMARY
(Erase heading not required.)

19

Place	Date	Hour	Summary of Events and Information	Remarks and references to Appendices
	Dec. 1915		The work of the R.E. 13th Div. during December 1915 may be summarised as follows:— (1) **Flooring trenches**: Lead gratings or board walk laid in C₂ Wellington Avenue 250 yds laid and another 300 yds. S of Arcadia Rue Pilkad nearly completed Rue Pilkad nearly completed Rue Pilkad nearly completed in King's Avenue, 250 yds D₁ 80a S of Arcadia D₃ 2 F₁ 50 yds laid in Bécourt Avenue laid in Aberdeen Avenue About 1000 yds laid in Bécourt Avenue E₂ 400 yds along Scunningham St E₃ 60 yds laid St Andrew's Avenue 600 yds bricked Perth Avenue W — 400 yds bricked (2) **Pumps** issued for pumping out low lying places.	

SECRET

WAR DIARY of COY 1st D.S.
INTELLIGENCE SUMMARY
(Erase heading not required.)

Army Form C. 2118

Place	Date	Hour	Summary of Events and Information	Remarks and references to Appendices
	Dec 1915		(3) Shelters — 21 completed.	
			(4) Lighting and Heating — 105 stoves and 64 lamps have been received and issued to units.	
			(5) Bomb stores — Three in hand. Box to hold bombs, lined with tin, are being made and issued. Box to hold bombs.	
			(6) Water supply. E.1. Pipe line laid to BECOURT CHATEAU and water laid on to 1400 gallon tank. E 2. & E 3 — Two large tanks erected and connected to pumping station.	
			(7) Comforts for troops. Progress has been made in providing wood accommodation, buildings and as under construction last month have been completed. In addition a Recreation Room 18'x 20' has been partially built & is being ____	
			(8) Repairs to trenches — Continual work has had to be put in during the month to keep the trenches fit for use. Continual fine weather has ____ a sudden fall of rain may tend to fall in	

20

SECRET

WAR DIARY
of C.R.E. 18th Div
INTELLIGENCE SUMMARY

Army Form C. 2118

Place	Date	Hour	Summary of Events and Information	Remarks and references to Appendices
	Dec 5/1915		(A) Repairs to roads. The road from BUIRE to BECOURT via DERNANCOURT, MEAULTE & BECORDEL is being broadened so as to admit of traffic in both directions.	21
			(10) Timber cutting. No. 16 Platoon R.E. Pioneers employed on cutting poplar fr saw bench at BONNAY HEILLY, and TREUX.	
			50 men of 18th Bn Cyclist Coy employed at ST GRATIEN in cutting brushwood, which is then made up into hurdles by special hurdle makers from Brigades.	

List of changes in officers to attached.

Lt Col CRE 18th Div
C.R.E. 18th Div

LIST OF CHANGES IN OFFICERS. R.E

18TH DIVISION.

NAME.	UNIT.	NATURE OF CHANGE.
Lt C.G.J.Kynam.	79th Field Coy.	Promoted Captain. 1.11.15.
2/Lt E.S.Rowe.	92nd Field Coy.	Joined 14.12.15.
Lt R.C.Christie.	80th Field Coy.	Killed 15/12/15.
Lt M.Wadeson.	92nd Field Coy.	Evacuated to Base Hospital 14/12/15.
2/Lt L.L.Viggers.	80th Field Coy.	Joined 20/12/15. vice Lt R.C Christie.
Capt F.J.M.King.	80th Field Coy.	Evacuated to No.5 C.C.S. on 29/12/15.

List of units attached in month

218th Coy. R.E. was attached for instruction from Decr 1st. 2 sections left 23.12.15 and the remainder leave on 2.1.16

23

WAR DIARY or INTELLIGENCE SUMMARY

Army Form C. 2118

SECRET

Head Quarters 18th Divl. Engineers

24

Place	Date	Hour	Summary of Events and Information	Remarks and references to Appendices
HEILLY	1.1.16 to 31.1.16		Work carried out by 79th, 80th and 92nd Field Companies as reported by them in their WAR DIARIES.—	
			H.Q.XVIII. The section of 80th Field Company engaged in improving hutment accommodation in the village by erecting two huts. Recd. from 583 mm erected during the month.— Work delayed for want of timber. Stores supplied. Scheme to lay on water from a spring south east of BUIRE to the ALBERT-AMIENS Road for horse standings on the BUIRE-LAVIEVILLE Road commenced.—	
			One section of 92nd Field Co. HS billeted at TREUX looking after C.R.E's men. Messing accommodation. Recd. for 280 additional men made. Buildings effected. New hut erected for H.Q.R.E. which that Signal Co. officers stat as office & C branch commenced.—	
			BUIVILLE-VIA-ANCRE bathing establishment manned by detachment of 92nd Field Co. One new hut 36' x 18' to act as a waiting room commenced	

SECRET

Army Form C. 2118

Sheet 2

WAR DIARY
or
INTELLIGENCE SUMMARY

(Erase heading not required.) Head Quarters 18th Divl Eng

Instructions regarding War Diaries and Intelligence
Summaries are contained in F. S. Regs., Part II.
and the Staff Manual respectively. Title Pages
will be prepared in manuscript.

Place	Date	Hour	Summary of Events and Information	Remarks and references to Appendices
HEILLY	1.1.16 to 31.1.16		and completed. Another hut 35'×12' for billets commenced. New machinery washing, drying & sterilising machines and shower bath have been erected. Workshop HEILLY continued to make Tables, Benches and water troughs –	
	19.1.16		At relief C.M.S.C. SENLIS to see C.M.S. 32. Division re F₁ and F₂	
	22.1.16 23.1.16		Reconnaissance of F₁ & F₂.	ALS

N.H. Jackolliniere
Major R.E.
C.R.E. 18th Division
3.1.16

25

SECRET

WAR DIARY
or
INTELLIGENCE SUMMARY

Army Form C. 2118

Head Quarters R.E. 18th Division

(Erase heading not required.)

Place	Date	Hour	Summary of Events and Information	Remarks and references to Appendices
HEILLY	1.1.16 to 31.1.16		Extracts from B 213	
			Major A. O. Walker R.E. left on 13.1.16 to join 48th Division.	
			No 52150 Driver W Thompson transferred to 48th Division 17.1.16	
			Major W. L. Lees R.E. to HQ.rs 18th Divl Eng vice Major A.O. Walker 16.1.16	
			No 49479 Driver T Povey transferred from 92° Field Co to 16.11.00.rs 16.1.16	
			Lt Col H. G. T. de Lotbinière on leave from 18.1.16 to 26.1.16. Major W. L. Lees R.E. acting as CRE between these dates.	Notes Major
			Capt E H Crump R.E. who had been Asst to CRE 18th Division returned and reported to CRE 1st Corps 31.1.16.	

N. [Lotbinière]
Lt Col RE
CRE 18th Division

26

C.R.E.
18th Div
Vol. 5.

27

WAR DIARY or INTELLIGENCE SUMMARY

Army Form C. 2118

HQRE 18 Div

18TH DIVN.   5 - MAR. 1916

Place	Date	Hour	Summary of Events and Information	Remarks and references to Appendices
Ribemont	1st February		Divisional School of Instruction. The work entailed the provision of Lecture Hall, complete with forms, tables, blackboard 8'0" x 10'0". Officers, men & furniture, 3 O.C's	
	2nd February		Portable Huts 8'0" x 10'0" for accommodation of Officers and installation H.C.O's Mess and accommodation with sanitation and beds complete. Officers Kitchen, 9 C.O's and mens kitchen. Water Supply, Drainage etc.	
			Bde. H.Q. provided for 54th Bde Brigade	
			BUIRE Water Supply completed as for an D.A.C. lines BUIRE Between to AMIENS - ALBERT Road construction.	
			80th Fld Coy R.E. proceeded to NAOURS on 3/2/16. Undertake expd units	
			148th A.T. Coy joined 5/2/16	
			1 Section 92nd Coy R.E. proceeded to 3rd Army School, FLEXICOURT 6 3/16	
			H.Q. R.E. moved from HEILLY to RIBEMONT on 6/2	
			Major Lees R.E. on leave from 8th to 15th	
			Lt. Waddson R.E. joined 24/2 transferred to 80th Coy R.E.	
			from Leeds left to assume command 3rd Porolying Company 27/2	
			Capt C.Y. Steadman R.E. assumed duties of Adjutant H.C.R.E. on 27/16	

28

CRE 18 Div Vol 6

WAR DIARY
INTELLIGENCE SUMMARY

Army Form C. 2118

Head Quarters R.E.
18th Division

Place	Date	Hour	Summary of Events and Information	Remarks and references to Appendices
In the Field	March 6		Head Quarters, 18th Divisional R.E. moved from RIBEMONT to MONTIGNY.	
	6th to 20th		Division on rest.	
	20th		Divisional H.Q. R.E. moved to ETINEHEM	
	21st		Capt. C.J. Stevenson on leave to England.	

C.J. Stevenson
Capt R.E.
for CRE 18th Div.

D.A.G.
The Base

Army Form C. 2118.

WAR DIARY
or
INTELLIGENCE SUMMARY
(Erase heading not required.)

R.E. Vol 7. 8

C.R.E.
30 MAY 1916
18TH DIVN.

Place	Date	Hour	Summary of Events and Information	Remarks and references to Appendices
In Field	1st April		Capt. Cyfflewmson R.E. returned from leave from U.K.	
"	9th April		Lt. W.H. Baddeley, 8th R. Sussex Pioneers, attached H.Q. R.E. on leave to U.K.	
"	10th		Bois des TAILLES Well supply scheme commenced. Work consisted in installing engine & pumps on bank of River Somme on ETINEHEM-CHIPILLY Road, laying 1000 yards 4" main to Reservoir in Bois des TAILLES, constructing Storage Reservoir with a 10,000 gallon capacity, 3 supply mains 3" to various points, erection of horse troughs, standpipes etc.	
"	18th		Lt. W.H. Baddeley 8th R. Sussex Pioneers from leave in U.K. Lt. Col. H.G.J. de Fotteniere, C.R.E. on leave to U.K.	
"	20th		Divisional Camp out of line and went into Rest Camp at CAVILLON	
"	29th		79th Field Company R.E. remained in line for special work	
"	30th		Lt. Col. H.G.J. de Fotteniere returned from leave in U.K. Lieut Lewmam Capt. R.E. 1st Durham for 9th R.E. 18th Divn.	30

2449 Wt. W14957/M90 750,000 1/16 J.B.C. & A. Form/C.2118/12.

WAR DIARY or INTELLIGENCE SUMMARY

Army Form C. 2118.

C.R.E.
30 MAY 1916
18TH DIVN.

Place	Date	Hour	Summary of Events and Information	Remarks and references to Appendices
In the Field	May 1st		R.E. Head Quarters moved from ETINEHEM to CHIPILLY	
	10th		Initial Scheme for Bois des TAILLES Water Supply completed. Pump & Engine installed, 1000 yards 4" main laid, 10,000 gallon concrete reservoir constructed, 3 - 3" mains from Reservoir laid 350 ft. of haughing completed.	
	15th		Extension to Bois des TAILLES Water Scheme completed this consisted of 2 Storage tanks & 3" branch to Guards Entrenching Battalion from said trench installed at R.E. workshops CHIPILLY.	
	23rd			
	24th		Further extension of above water supply scheme completed work consisted in laying 1½" main & erecting storage tank for R.E. Balloon Section newly arrived	
	25th		Further entrenchments in hand	
	31st		Two sawbenches at R.E. workshops H.Q. are turning out sawn timber of various dimensions at rate of 70,000 ft. run per month.	

Sgd. Lieutenant R.E.
a/Capt. C.R.E. 18th Divn
for C.R.E. 18 th Divn

Army Form W.3091.

Cover for Documents.

Nature of Enclosures.

War Diaries
of
R.E. H.Q., 18 Div.

Period 1st April to June 1916

Notes, or Letters written.

SECRET

Army Form C. 2118

WAR DIARY
or
INTELLIGENCE SUMMARY

(Erase heading not required.)

Place	Date	Hour	Summary of Events and Information	Remarks references to Appendices
CHIPILLY.	21/6.	11am	Headquarters was transferred on this day from CHIPILLY to 18th Divisional Battle Headquarters close to and on the N. side of BRAY.	
	19/6.		The 90th Field Company, Royal Engineers was placed at the disposal of the 18th Division for work under the C.R.E from this day. A party from this Field Company relieved a platoon of the 8th Royal Sussex Pioneers under Lieut Capper at the CHIPILLY Workshops and Sawbenches.	
B.H.Q.	24/6.		The Bombardment of enemy positions and cutting of wire commenced on this day.	
B.H.Q.	25/6.		C.R.Es Operation Order published. Copy No.17 attached hereto.	No.17.

Adjutant, 18th Divisional Engineers.

Captain.R.E.
(S.R.)

Copy No. 17   36

... DIVISION ORDER No.1.   26th June, 1916

INFORMATION   1. (a) Enemy. The hostile trenches opposite the front of
                    the ... Division consist of :-
                    (i) Fire trench and support trench.
                    (ii) In rear of these, the line or POMMIER'S
                         REDOUBT.
                    (iii) The defended village of MONTAUBAN and
                          POMMIER'S REDOUBT.

              (b) Our own troops. The 30th Division is on our right.
                  The 7th Division IVth Corps is on our left.
                  The 9th Division is in Corps Reserve.

INTENTION   2. ... capture and consolidation of the objectives
                  ... from ... the front day's operations ...
                  ... preparations
                  ... for a further advance.
                  In order that this operation may be successfully
                  carried out it will be necessary for the 18th Division
                  to hold the line of its furthest objective for at least
                  ... day without being relieved.

EXECUTION   3. (a) FIELD COMPANIES
                     Field Companies (less 2 sections) will be under
                     the orders of the Brigadiers to whom they are
                     attached, for the consolidation of captured
                     positions.
                     The remaining sections will be employed as follows:-
                     79th Field Company - One section for repairing
                     CARNOY - MONTAUBAN Road. To begin work one hour
                     after 'ZERO' time.
                     80th Field Company - One section for maintenance
                     of BOZAGUE - CARNOY Water Supply.
                     92nd Field Company - One section for repairs to
                     CARNOY - MONTAUBAN Railway. To begin work two hours
                     after 'ZERO' time.
                     One section of each Field Company will be held in
                     Divisional Reserve and will move into CARNOY 3 hours
                     after 'ZERO' time.

              (b) PIONEERS
                  The 8th Royal Sussex Pioneers will make the
                  following dispositions:-
                  (i) Two platoons per Brigade to work with the R.E.
                      sections under the orders of Brigadiers.
                  (ii) One platoon to work on the CARNOY - MONTAUBAN
                       Road with the 79th Company. To be in work ...
                       ... 'ZERO' time.
                  (iii) One Company to open up Nos. 1, 2, 5 & 6 saps
                        in NO MAN'S LAND. To begin work one hour after
                        'ZERO' time, and to take over the remaining
                        saps Nos. 3, 4, 7 & 8 from the O.C., 183rd
                        Tunnelling Company at 9 pm on "Z" day.

Sheet 2. Copy No....

ORDERS TO 3 (Con.)
TROOPS
    (b) Pioneers (con.)
        (iv) The remaining 3 platoons to be held in Divisional
           Reserve and to move into CARNOY 3 hours after
           Zero time.

    (c) Army Troops Company
        The 230th Army Troops Company, R.E (less 2 sections)
        will be employed on the CARNOY – MONTAUBAN RO.D
        between CARNOY and our front line.
        They should reach CARNOY one hour after Zero time.
        This Company will bivouac in CARNOY on Z night and
        after.

DRESS AND 4 The following will be carried by all except specialists
EQUIPMENT. for whom special orders may be issued.
    (i) Rifle and equipment less pack.
    (ii) 120 rounds S.A.A.
    (iii) Haversack on the back, containing two tins of meat
        and eight hard biscuits and canteen packed with
        grocery ration.
    (iv) Waterproof sheet.
    (v) Jersey.
    (vi) Two Smoke Helmets.
    (vii) ....
    (viii) Packs will be stored under Company arrangements.

TRANSPORT 5 Field Company Transport will remain in their present
lines.
Field Company wagons will be bonded and parked in Divisional
Dump in readiness to take up R.E. Stores. These will
be sent forward to the lines when required.

DUMPS 6 In addition to the Forward and Brigade Dumps, a Corps
Dump will be formed in CARNOY. Lieutenant BRAITHWAITE,
of the Seaforth Highlanders (Pioneers) will be in charge.
Stores can be drawn after Zero time by Company of
Pioneers if required upon the signature of an officer.
The Divisional Dump in BRAY will remain at its present
for transferring stores from Lorries to Carts.

                                                C......L.......
                        Commanding Royal Engineers, 18th Division.

37

18 Divn

Vol 10

18/C.RE
July/16

18 Divn

WAR DIARY or INTELLIGENCE SUMMARY

Army Form C. 2118

(Erase heading not required.)

Place: [illegible]
Date: 1st July 1916
Hour:

Summary of Events and Information

The whole of the Divisional Engineers were employed during the operation on the Somme during the early part of July as stated under various heads.

a/ Water supply.

The SUZANNE - CARNOY water supply was maintained by a section of 1st Field Coy. Water was on the Divisional area was included. It delivery on various new land so far as "POMMIER REDOUBT" as it was completed to the German system. By this water was brought up to and including MONTAUBAN ALLEY + various points as CATERPILLAR RAVINE & along O.G.1 & 16th 17th after Caches on to the 5.5 ere the officers concerned.

b/ Roads.

1. During the early stages of the operation the CARNOY - MONTAUBAN road was placed in a satisfactory state of repair, also the first deviation made also the rear deviation from the cemetery Carnoy towards... The work was carried out by a detachment of the 5th Pl coy, a platoon of Pioneers and for a short time of 238th AT Cy under Capt Evans B/ Coy 15th on 20th KLR state of the work was handed over to the CRE 111rd Division
The routes were found the traffic from BRONFAY FARM to CARNOY were the
2.00 Whole area were constructed from BRONFAY FARM to CARNOY are one main thence : a) 10 miles of CARNOY WOOD and LA GUERRE WOOD

WAR DIARY or INTELLIGENCE SUMMARY

Army Form C. 2118

39

3) Our the western front (BERNAFAY WOOD and TRONES WOOD), the Division continued to work on the BRIQUETERIE ROAD and the relief of 21st & 5th Divns. at Montauban — Carnoy & 30th Division Relief.

4) Our losses as stated from MACHINE GUN WOOD to SE corner of TRONES WOOD. 23 Other ranks wounded. Traffic on the BRIQUETERIE road...

c) **Railways**
The R.O.D. 8" gun railway line from CARNOY to MONTAUBAN was being further 8" employed as far as dump behind cable station — extra 8" of 92" Cable [?] consists of 3 linemen from 1 Divnl. Sig. Coy. front line a... contact of men after our advance to fill up between S. [...] monitors in [?]

d) **Consolidation**
That the defensive works are still being objective of RE works. All the front field work, the details of traces from Bernafay O.10 One Coy front of strong Coy line was contrasted on E edge of BERNAFAY WOOD not along front are [shelled] — TRONES WOOD.

e) Other communications – ... Reserve Safe at "down" ... R.D. Rail

WAR DIARY
or
INTELLIGENCE SUMMARY

Army Form C. 2118

Date	Hour	Summary of Events and Information	Remarks and references to Appendices
1-12/7/16		Recce report by 18th Divn G.S. under Major Hood, RE were opened at 5 a.m. copies of the Report sent Divn. 6th army & 10 gun mines of the Divn. opened. Major Kirwin. RE Supt. are boring out spoil obstacles now known to exist at CATERPILLAR TRENCH & EAST TRENCH	
13		f Details	
		The Bray cut out was conducted by Major Brown. CARNOY cut out second half by Major Beach in Group durn.	
14		On 14th a conference was held at MARICOURT a.a. to Gerald Gunter present durn to Improving road between BERNAFAY and TRONES WOOD	
		Headquarters at 18th Divn Headquarters N.E. of BRAY HQRE (Col. G. Rivers) moved to CORSE VALLEY Cpt Raden assumed duties of Asst-sec. via Cpt C.Y. Sebrouh so absent & regretted duty	
19		Hqrs. opened at BRAY	
21		" " AMIENCOURT	
26		" " TENESCURE	
31st		Or/fff by 11th CRE operations on front of CROIX du BAC on that Divisional Front S.E. of ARMENTIÈRES CRE NZ Divn now so act	

40

Army Form C. 2118

CRE from 1/8W folio. V&17

WAR DIARY
or
INTELLIGENCE SUMMARY

(Erase heading not required.)

18th Divl. 1 C.E. H.Q.   AUGUST. 1916.

Place	Date	Hour	Summary of Events and Information	Remarks and references to Appendices
Croix du Bac	1st		H.Q. at Croix du Bac.	
	2nd 3rd 4th		Field Companies inspected by E.O.C. 18th Div. & Sr IAN CAPPER.	
	5th 6th		Taking over new Divisional Front from CRE. N.Z. Div. (II ANZAC CORPS) workshops Dumps Temporary bridges RE Field Companies. Transport at ERQUINHAM. 79th Field Co. RE ERQUINHAM. 80th " Pont MARAIS 92nd " S. PRES PT 2 Sections 79th RE detailed for work with R.F.A. Dumps wirelephone (2 seds) for 4 Brigade fronts for R & 5°. Run put as above.	41
	7th	2.30		
	2.55. 28th 21st		Handing over to CRE. 34th Div. HQ moved to 38 ARTILLERY	Ulhawicke off. RE 18 Div. RE

Army Form C. 2118

WAR DIARY

Intelligence Summary
(Erase heading not required.)

No. 2
August 1916.
18th Dn. R.E. H.Q.

Place	Date	Hour	Summary of Events and Information	Remarks and references to Appendices
BAILLEUL	25th		H.Q. Entrained for St Pol; and moved into billets at BOIRAN.	
BOIRAN	26th / 31st		DIVISIONAL TRAINING :— Consolidation of captured Trenches & to & ground & & woods. Intensive Rifle & Rapid Fire. Tunnelled O.Ps were cut/dug and Pit/emplacements. Company Training Musketry	
	26th		Capt T.B. HARRIS has R.E. ICE and Coys attached command of 79th Field Co R.E. vice Temp. Lieut Col. CRE to 25th Division MAJOR DONE appointed.	
	28th			

R.W. Chambers
Capt. Regt R.E.
18th Dn. R.E.

42

WAR DIARY or INTELLIGENCE SUMMARY

Army Form C. 2118

WO RE-18A Vol 12

43

Place	Date	Hour	Summary of Events and Information	Remarks and references to Appendices
BOIRAN	Sept 1st to Sept 9th		CRE HQ at BOIRIN. Division in training in MONCHY-BOSTON TRAINING AREA under administration of XVII Corps. Field Companies engaged in training and instruction of Infantry in Rapid wiring, rapid consolidation including rapid dug-out construction and sufficient wiring.	
BOULLENS	" 9th		H.Q. RE. moved to BOULLENS closing at BOIRAN at 8.15 am opening at BOULLENS at 9.30 am	
ACHEUX	" 11th		H.Q. RE moved to ACHEUX	
	16-20		Companies RE continued to train with Brigades in rapid consolidation	
	22nd		79th and 80th Companies RE moved from LEAVILLERS to MARTINSAART area together with THIEPVAL AREA. 92nd RE in DIVISIONAL RESERVE and occupied in proving billeting accommodation and hutting in ACHEUX	
	23rd Oct		Work to organisation of RE Dumps, tramways, water supply etc affecting operation against THIEPVAL	
MESNIEVILLE	25th 26th		H.Q. RE moved from ACHEUX closing at 9 am opening at MESNIEVILLE at 11 am. Operations against THIEPVAL, village captured	
	27th–28th		Operations against SCHWABEN Redoubt	
	30th		92nd RE moved from ACHEUX to MARTINSAART to take over from 105th RE work on Water Supply, Tramways etc	
			Casualties in DURSIGNY RE during month :— 1 Officer killed in action Lieut. J.F. WILSON, T.C. 79th RE 1 Officer wounded in action i/T, R.T.O. PAGE 80th RE 2 O.R. killed and 21 wounded in action	

Wt. W593/826 1,000,000 4/15 J.B.C. & A. A.D.S.S./Forms/C. 2118.

Army Form C. 2118

WAR DIARY
or
INTELLIGENCE SUMMARY
(Erase heading not required.)

Instructions regarding War Diaries and Intelligence Summaries are contained in F. S. Regs., Part II. and the Staff Manual respectively. Title Pages will be prepared in manuscript.

folio. v.

Place	Date	Hour	Summary of Events and Information	Remarks and references to Appendices
	17th Sept		CAPT. C.G.J. LYNAM. (T.C.) to command 108th Field Co. R.E. LIEUT. R.E. KNIGHT (S.R.) to second in command of 79th Field Co R.E. from 92nd Field Co. R.E. to succeed CAPT. C.G.J. LYNAM. (T.C.)	
	26th Sept		" LIEUT. R.G. DYER (T.C.) posted to 92nd Field Co R.E. from BAFC.	
	23rd Sept		" LIEUT. R.C. FINCH (T.C.) Transferred to 135th A.T. Co R.E. Authority H.Q. Res Army AC/9448 19/9/16.	

B.W. Lambert
Capt. Adjt. R.E.
18th Division.

HH

Army Form C. 2118.

WAR DIARY
or
INTELLIGENCE SUMMARY.
(Erase heading not required.)

HQ RE 18 D Vol 13

45

Place	Date	Hour	Summary of Events and Information	Remarks and references to Appendices
	OCT		H.Q. - 18th DIVISION - RE	(1.)
HERMAVILLE	1st - 5th		18th Division holding Schwaben Redoubt Sector.	
BERNAVILLE	6th		H.Q. 18th Div RE moved back to BERNAVILLE handing over to 39th Div RE.	
"	12th - 13th		79th Co. Transport left for area en route to ALBERT via HERRLISART with 53rd Bde.	
"	15		79th Co. Personnel to ALBERT by lorry. NOTE: 80th and 92nd Field Coys left for "K" area yesterday with 54th and 55th Bdes.	
ALBERT	16		HQ. moved from 'Q' area to ALBERT.	
"	19		67th and 68th Field Companies RE attached for duty.	
"	21		53rd Bde attacked REGINA TRENCH 79th Co RE attached. Operations entirely successful.	
TARA HILL	22		HQ moved from ALBERT to TARA HILL 1500' S.W. of LA BOISELLE	
"	25		219th Field Company RE attached for duty.	
"	31		Site arranged for NISSEN BOW HUT Camp. 40 huts to be erected 700 yards S.W. of OVILLERS-LA-BOISELLE on road to AVELUY. 3 Sick of Flu. Need	

Army Form C. 2118.

WAR DIARY
or
INTELLIGENCE SUMMARY.
(Erase heading not required.)

Instructions regarding War Diaries and Intelligence Summaries are contained in F.S. Regs., Part II. and the Staff Manual respectively. Title pages will be prepared in manuscript.

Place	Date	Hour	Summary of Events and Information	Remarks and references to Appendices
TARA HILL			H.Q. 18 Division. R.E.	
			Work in hand during period 16th – 31st Oct. 1916.	
			(i) Road through POZIERES running N. to R.34.c. Clearing, draining, coduroying and metalling.	
			(ii) Road from POZIERES to COURCELETTE through R.35 central. 5°	
			(iii) Maintenance and running of Tramline from POZIERES to R.29. central.	
			(iv) Constructing and running of Tramline from R.33.d.9.2 to R.28.b. 1400ˣ laid.	
			(v) Track gridded from X.a.d.2.8 to R.34.d.2.4. 800 yards.	
			5° R.33.d.7.3 to R.33.b.3.8. 800 "	
			(vi) 5° " R.34.c. central to R.29 central.	
			(vii) Mule track from X.4 central to R.29 central.	
			(viii) Clearing, cleaning and gridding main communication trenches.	
			(ix) Clearing and repairing Dug-outs (Bosch): and construction of new ones.	
			(x) Formation of Divisional C.G. Dump at X.9.6.8.	
			(xi) Repair of Artillery Bridges.	
			(xii) Construction of Prisoners Cage at R.29.a.	
			(xiii) R.A.M.C. Collecting Station at R.29.a.	
			(xiv) NISSEN Bow huting scheme for 1 Battalion commenced 700ˣ S.W. of OVILLERS on AVELUY ROAD.	

46

Army Form C. 2118.

WAR DIARY
or
INTELLIGENCE SUMMARY.
(Erase heading not required.)

Place	Date	Hour	Summary of Events and Information	Remarks and references to Appendices
HQ 18th Divl. Cdy.			(3)	
			Divisional RE Casualties.	
			Wounded and still at duty. 3. O.R.	
			Wounded 14. O.R. 2 Officers.	
			Killed 1 O.R.	
			Reinforcement 15. O.R. 2 Officers.	
			Horses Evacuated 1. R. & L.D.	
				B.C.Chambers
				Capt R.E.
				Adj. 18th Divl. R.E.

47

WAR DIARY
or
INTELLIGENCE SUMMARY

48

Place	Date	Hour	Summary of Events and Information	Remarks and references to Appendices
H.Q. TARA HILL ALBERT.	Nov 1st	-	18th Division R.E. Attached units 67th Field Co R.E. (11th Bde) 68th " " (") 219th " " (53rd Bde) And assistance given by 1st Field Squadron R.E.	
	6th		1st Field Squadron left area.	
	7th 12		8 11th Division R.Es Wagons attached to Pioneer	
	8th		3 18th " " " to 79th R.E. } to forward road works	
	9th 12		" " " RAC Wagon }	
			10 15th Reserve Park Wagon to Pioneers	
	11th 12		No 3 Section 174th Tunneling Company R.E. attached for duty	
	12th 12		219th Field Company R.E. returned to 32nd Division for duty	
	13th 12		68th Field Company R.E. to 19th Division for duty	
	15th 12		No. 4 Section 174th Tunneling Company R.E. attached for duty	
			3 Officers and 65 O.R. T.M.B. 18th Divn ARTILLERY attached for duty, cutting brushwood (for infantry routes) in Caterpillar Wood	
	17th 12		67th Field Co. R.E. returned to 11th Division for duty	Elladuits Copt R.E. Left 12th Div - E.E.
	20		3/1st and 2/2nd Midland Field Companies R.E. attached for duty from 6th Divn	
	21st		1/3rd Midland Field Company R.E. attached for duty from 6th Division	

Army Form C. 2118.

WAR DIARY
or
INTELLIGENCE SUMMARY.
(Erase heading not required.)

Place	Date	Hour	Summary of Events and Information	Remarks and references to Appendices
HQ TARA HILL	Nov. 22nd		18th Division moved back to training area and Pioneers to remain in line one week to assist 6th Division.	(2)
ALBERT	28th		No. 3 and 4 Sections 174th Tunneling Company RE transferred to 6th Div. Handing over to 6th Division completed.	
	30th		Proposed to rejoin Division in next few towards complete. All arrangements cancelled, RE and Pioneers to remain formed and to work on Corps line. Reconnaissance of Pottestine commenced.	

49

Army Form C. 2118.

WAR DIARY
or
INTELLIGENCE SUMMARY.
(Erase heading not required.)

Instructions regarding War Diaries and Intelligence Summaries are contained in F. S. Regs., Part II. and the Staff Manual respectively. Title pages will be prepared in manuscript.

Place	Date	Hour	Summary of Events and Information	Remarks and references to Appendices
HQ. TARA-HILL ALBERT.	Nov		18th Battalion RE	
			Work in hand during the month.	
			(i) Road through POZIERES running N. & S. R.34.c. drained and metalled	
			(ii) " from POZIERES to COURCELETTE R.26 central continued and metalled over damaged cover.	
			(iii) Maintenance road running frontline from TULLOCH'S CORNER R.33.d.8.3 to R.22.d.1.5. 2000' laid	
			(iv) Maintenance and running frontline from POZIERES R.29. central	
			(v) Track jidded from MOUQUET FARM to RED TRENCH 500"	
			(vi) " " " " bush wood " 1200"	
			(vii) " " REGINA TRENCH FOSSÉE R.21.B.5.4 - R.16.d.9.8.	
			(viii) Clearing cleaning main communication and holding same.	
			(ix) Clearing and repairing trenches they all and construction of new dug out	
			(x) Formation of DIVISION RE DUMP at TULLOCH'S CORNER R.33.d.8.5	
			(xi) Construction of NISSEN Bow HUT Camp at X.7.a.6.2 to X.13.a.9.8. 20 huts erected	
			(xii) Commencement of another NISSEN Bow HUT Camp at X.1.d.1.1. 3 huts erected. Foundations laid for 10 additional.	
			One Section RE. 18th BULLONIAN SCHOOL to construct same near ARROUVILLE	

50

WAR DIARY
or
INTELLIGENCE SUMMARY.

Army Form C. 2118.

(Erase heading not required.)

Place	Date	Hour	Summary of Events and Information	Remarks and references to Appendices
HQ TARA HILL ALBERT	Nov.		18th Divisional Rft.	(4)
			Divisional Rft. Casualties	
				Officers OR
			Wounded and Evacuated wd. wd.	
			Wounded + Evacuated " 1 5	
			Killed wd. —	
			Shell Shock " wd. wd.	
			To hospital Sick " 2 9	
			Reinforcements " x 11	
			Iron hospital " wd. 4	
			Horse Evacuated R wd. L.D. 5	
			Reinforcement wd. 5	

Ablabue.
Capt. R.E.
Adjt. 18th Div. R.E.

51

WAR DIARY or INTELLIGENCE SUMMARY

Army Form C. 2118

F.290.
Vol 15

Place	Date	Hour	Summary of Events and Information	Remarks and references to Appendices
NR. SARA WOOD ALBERT	Dec 1st	19h	18th Div. R.E. H.Q. Field Companies attached to CRE Wellington for work under 4th Corps.	
CHATEAU ONVILLE	8th		R.E. H.Q. moved back to II Corps Training Area. Organising training and billeting schemes.	
	31st			
	22nd		Field Companies arrived back in Training Area. Looking to erection of huts and improvement of billets.	

B.C.H. Ambrose.
Captain.
Adjt. 18th Div. R.E.

WAR DIARY or INTELLIGENCE SUMMARY

Army Form C. 2118

WORE 182 Vol 16

53

Place	Date	Hour	Summary of Events and Information	Remarks and references to Appendices
OUVILLE	Jan 1st	-	C.R.E. 18th DIVISION.	
	" 11	-	Companies engaged on hutting and improvements to Billets in BUSSY AREA.	
	" 12	-	" marched to forward area.	
	" 13	-	Handed over hutting and billet improvement work to C.R.E. 5th Div. and moved BERNAVILLE	
BERNAVILLE	" 14	-	H.Q. at BERNAVILLE	
	" 15	-	Ditto moved to MARIEUX	
MARIEUX	" 16	-	-	
BOUZINCOURT		-	Moved to BOUZINCOURT. Took over from C.R.E. 51st DIVISION.	R.E.Rainbow Capt & Adjt
			79)	Capt Edwards
			80) Field Coys. R.E. in line	
			91) " " in Support Area.	
			Work on Communication trenches. Forward Tramway. Extension and repair. Dugouts. cleaning and repairing. Erection of Nissen huts. Repairs and extensions to Camp, huts and Aveluy wood cutting. Erection of Baths	
	31st			

WAR DIARY
or
INTELLIGENCE SUMMARY

Army Form C. 2118

HQ 18th Divn. R.E.

54

During the month February the CRE's Head Quarters were at Bouzincourt with Head Quarters of Division. Conference in Battalion and dugouts in forward area. 79th & 80th Coys. took part in attack on P. Mesnil and trench on Feb. 17th during which operation L/Corporal Smith was killed whilst laying out advanced starting point. During subsequent operation died. Byes the 92nd Coy. was killed. Remainder of the month the Companies were chiefly employed in important communication work owing to the German retirement and to Achiet le Petit line. Much work was done on the St. Pierre Divion - Bauvcourt - Miraumont road which had become impassable through the effect of shell fire, and which was the only available road when called to assist the Artillery. During the month one Company was entirely employed in improvement to trench hutted etc. erection of bath houses, recreation hut - Church Army hut in the Support Brigade area.

L. Hayne Lt. R.E.
Acting Adjutant
18th Divn. Engineers

ORDER No.1.

OPERATION ORDERS
by
LIEUT COLONEL H.M.HENDERSON R.E., C.R.E., 18TH DIVISION

Headquarters.R.E.,

18th Division.

Ref.ANCRE
VALLEY MAP
1/10,000

16th February,1917.

1. Strong points will be made in the following localities :-
   (i) 50 to 75 yards W. of WEST MIRAUMONT ROAD at R.11.a.9.0.
   (ii) Below the crest at R.11.a.1.3.
   (iii) At the point of the spur at R.10.b.4.5.
   (iv) On the railway at R.10.a.4.7.
   (v) On the BOOM Ravine at R.11.c.2.5.
   (vi) On the bank, in which are dugouts, at R.10.d.4.7.

   2nd Division will make a strong point on the South side of the BOOM Ravine at R.11.d.0.4 which will have a machinegun sited to support our strong points (v) & (vi) by firing across their front along the northern slope of the ravine.

2. Strong points are allotted as follows :-
   (i),(ii) & (v) to 80th Field Co.R.E.
   (iii),(iv) & (vi) to 79th Field Co.R.E.

   These strong points will be made by the sections of R.E., with their attached infantry and machine gun crew. They will on completion garrison them until taken over by the Infantry of the Brigade in whose sector they are situated.
   These strong points should consist of a machine gun sited to fire in the direction pointed out to Os.C.Companies on the map and should be adapted to the ground. They should take the form of a crucifix or a "Z" or some type which is not circular and adapted for all round defence.
   As far as possible their front stretch of wire should be enfiladed by the gun on the right or the left and the firebays for the Infantry designed to protect the gun itself.
   The garrison will consist of a machine gun and some twenty men.
   These strong points should be designed to be made within six hours of arrival on the ground.

3. Field Company Commanders will arrange with their Brigadiers for the formation of the necessary R.E.Dumps for these strong points.

4. The orders for the advance of these sections and the attached infantry and machine gun crew, will come from the respective Brigadiers under whom the Company usually works ; who have orders not to order their advance until the objective in front of the proposed strong points is captured. As soon as the strong point is finished a message is to be sent to the Brigadiers of the Brigades concerned, who have orders to arrange for their garrisoning, also to the C.R.E. and as soon as the points are garrisoned the sections can return to their respective locations and rest, awaiting further orders.

5. The 92nd Field Co.R.E. will furnish one section and the attached infantry to work on the water supply : one section and attached infantry to work on the SAINT PIERRE DIVION ROAD and one section on the A.T.N Divisional Dump.

6. The three reserve sections and the attached infantry will work on "Z" day on the new railway from OVILLERS TOWN to RIFLE DUMP somewhere in the locality of RIFLE DUMP. The names of the officers in charge of these sections should be reported to the C.R.E under whose orders they directly are. They are not to be employed on other work by Company Commanders without reference to the C.R.E.

Para.7.

Page 2.OO.No.1.

7. Units should report exact localities of their H.Q and sections as soon as they are definitely settled.

8. The 8th Royal Sussex Pioneers will be employed entirely on completing the railway from OVILLERS TOWN to ROGERS LINE and forward, and in keeping all the railways in a state of repair.

9. Advanced Divisional R.E.Dump will be formed at RIFLE DUMP, reference C.R.E.Circular Memorandum No.6. Lieut Griffith R.E will take charge of the dump and also the Divisional reserve dump at O.T.
    The N.C.O in charge of RIFLE Dump will issue stores on the signatures of Os.C.R.E.Sections : and will demand stores to be sent up from O.T to replace.

10. Six pontoon wagons will be parked at AVELUY DUMP, with stores which can be forwarded by road to COURCELETTE or GRANDCOURT as demanded by Company Commanders who must provide guides.

11. For Tramway arrangements see C.R.E letter No.20/5/8.

12. ACKNOWLEDGE.

R.W.Chambers

Captain.R.E.

Adjutant, 18th Divisional Engineers.

Issued at 11.am.

Distribution :-

    Field Companies.R.E.
    O.i/c A.T.N.R.E.Dump.
    8th Royal Sussex Pioneers.
    18th Division G.
    18th Division A/Q.
    War Diary.
    File.

"B"
57

ORDERS
by
LIEUT COLONEL H.M.HENDERSON,R.E., C.R.E., 19th DIVISION

ORDER NO.2.

Headquarters R.E.,
19th Division.
20th February, 1917.

1. The following changes of locations of billets will take place on the 21st Instant. Companies will report completion of change by wire to this office, changes of work to take place on the 22nd Instant inclusive.

2. Work on GRANDCOURT ROAD will be executed from BRIDGE ROAD forward, by Serial No. C plus 4 companies of infantry already detailed in C.R.E's letter 21/4/3.

3. The 80th Field Company will complete the Baths at CRUCIFIX CORNER, the erection of the CHURCH ARMY Hut at WELLINGTON Huts, also supervise the flooring of GLOSTER Huts, in addition to supervising O.K.Dump, Divisional Workshops and Divisional Dump, AVELEY, with men from serial No. B plus two daily platoons from the Division already detailed in C.R.E's letter No.21/4/3.

4. The O.C.,80th Company,R.E., will arrange with the O.C.,92nd Company,R.E., to take over and ration the 37 Infantry tradesmen working at the A.T.N.Dump.

5. Transport will be under the 80th Company,R.E., from the 22nd Instant inclusive.

6. Os. C Companies will arrange when handing over work that continuity is ensured.

7. Workshop special R.E details such as Engine Drivers, Sawyers, Storekeepers, etc., on the ration strength of Divisional H.Q.R.E. remain as before.

Captain.R.E.
Adjutant, 19th Divisional Engineers.

Issued at 10/40.p.m.

War Diary.

UNIT.	SERIAL NO.	STRENGTH.	WORK.	LOCATION
79th Co.	A.	2 sections. / 2 platoons. }	Work in the Line.	Company H.Q. at X.2.a.3.1. / X.2.a.3.1. }
	B.	2 sections. / 2 platoons. }	Tractor Line to ZOLLERN assisted by 174.Coy.	1 section } R.27.b. / 1 platoon } / 1 section. } R.21.central. / 1 platoon. }
80th Co.	C.	2 sections. / 2 platoons. }	GRANDCOURT ROAD.	Company H.Q. MIDLAND HUTS. / 1 section. } Q.24.b.8.2. / 1 section. } Midland Huts. 2 Plns McKenzie Huts.
	D.	1 section. / 1 platoon. }	Repair 4" main from BLIGHTY VALLEY to NAB JUNC.	Midland Huts.
	E.	1.section. / 1 platoon. }	R.E. Divisional Workshops and O.T.Dumps.	1 section } Midland Huts. / 1 platoon } McKenzie Huts. / Infantry } McKenzie Huts. / Tradesmen.}
92nd Co.	F.	2 sections. / 2 platoons. }	New 4" and 2" extension and tanks.	COMPANY H.Q. at X.2.a.1.4. / X.2.a.1.4. }
	G.	2 sections. / 2 platoons. }	Work in the Line.	RIFLE DUMP. Dugouts H.13,14,15, & 16.
		TRANSPORT.		3 Field Coys. W.9.b.9.5.

WAR DIARY
or
INTELLIGENCE SUMMARY

Army Form C. 2118.

CRE
18th Division
Vol 18

Place	Date	Hour	Summary of Events and Information	Remarks and references to Appendices
			From March 1st to 22nd the CRO was at Corps H.d. Q's. Hatford with Div. Head Quarters, moving from there to Bus near Amiens for two days en route for Steenbecque in the 2nd Army area. Previous to the attack in the area, on the 10th the Companies were employed on the following works. 79th Coy. repairs and improvement road through Sandcourt and Petit Miraumont. 80th Coy. Corduroy road from Miri Road Corner to Pan St. Pierre and improvement to Batts and Divisional Cadre at Aveling. 92nd Coy. Water Supply scheme. 93rd Coy. Sanitation and water table fillers. Section 1 the attack on 10th, the 79 & Coy. had 4 sections employed on advanced strong points and the 92nd Coy. had one section similarly employed there. 80th Coy made all arrangements and was occupied on infantry & M.G. positions south of Irles. The advanced field parks which had been brought up in support. From 18th to 20th one Company was fully employed in back area "Project Runway" Service and dumps and work at billets etc in rear. The Coy. who kept one section at work on maintenance of the frontal area toward Coy. were entirely occupied on road and rail traffic scheme. Road difficult was experienced in keeping the roads open to all traffic, B. Army to the continual steady traffic of all descriptions most of which was of the	C.R.E. Order No. 3. 8/3/17

59

nearest nature it was never possible to complete in proper before I was
used. The following roads were found not in fair condition: St Pierre Divion —
Monument; Monument — Irles; Lust and West Monument Road, and
the main road to Beheaucourt and Achiet le Grand — Gueudecourt tracks
were made from Monument to the four cross roads at G.22.c.5.3. To
take traffic off the main road.

Water supply schemes included maintenance of the hot Irancher - Boom
Ravine pipe line, which was constantly [indecipherable] and the provision and
[indecipherable] that the line was [indecipherable].

Advanced 2" pipe line was laid from the stopper at R.S.C.3.c in
P. Monument to an 800 gal tank in Standard Road and on to Irles.
During the subsequent advance the 85th Company provided 3 sections in
the Advance Guard and reconnoitred roads and water supplies and
much useful information was obtained. Samples of water were taken
from the [indecipherable] well close to mud [indecipherable] [indecipherable] did not shew poison any
tracks were made [indecipherable] before I could complete the work
Company, but holt down before I could complete the work
From 23rd to 28th the Head Quarters and Companies were [indecipherable] from Lille
Army Area to that of First Army.

Army Form C. 2118.

C.R.E.
18th DIVISION.

WAR DIARY
or
INTELLIGENCE SUMMARY

(Erase heading not required.)

Place	Date	Hour	Summary of Events and Information	Remarks and references to Appendices
			During a reconnaissance of the forward positions at Sole and Col. Lt M Henderson in Coy with Lieut C M Chancy the Royal Sussex Regan. was hit by a shell and killed the bulls who returned to his injuries not as. Major W M Stayman DSO RE acted as OC the 14th when Lieut Col. C B G Symons DSO RE arrived from the Base and took up the Command. Casualties in OR's during the month have very slight. The loss in LD horses has been severe, which can be accounted for by the very heavy nature of the work which they have called upon to perform. The weather conditions have also much against them	61

V Rupus Lieut RE
& Rupus Lieut RE
Adjutant 18th Divisional RE

SECRET   ORDER No.3.

OPERATION ORDERS BY LIEUT COLONEL H.M.HENDERSON R.E.,

COMMANDING ROYAL ENGINEER, 18TH DIVISION.

> Headquarters, R.E.,
>
> 18th Division.
>
> 8th March, 1917.

Ref. Special Map.
ACHIET. 1/10,000.

1. Copies of 53rd Infantry Brigade Order No.59 have been issued to all concerned.

2. Five strong points are to be constructed by a section, Royal Engineers and their attached Infantry. *each*
   The location of these strong points is as follows :-
   (i). G.32.b.10.3.
   (ii). G.32.b.6.6.
   (iii). In or near trench about G.26.d.8.2.
   (iv). In sunken road about G.26.c.7.4½.
   (v). On or near where trench crosses the road, (suspected BOSCHE strong point) about G.25.b.9½.1½.

3. Strong points will also be constructed by the Infantry as follows :-
   (vi). In ravine about G.26.d.5.4.
   (vii). In quarry about G.26.c.3½.6½.
   (viii). On bank about G.32.a.8.9.

4. Strong points 1, 2, & 4 are to contain machine guns and the siting of these strong points is to be chiefly with reference to the flanking fire that must be obtained from these positions. The directions for the arcs of fire and instructions as to these have been issued to those concerned.
   Strong points 3 and 5 are for all round defence, fire being chiefly required in a direction from N.W to N.E.
   Strong points should not be circular but may be of the "Z" or Crucifix type.

5. It should be possible to tape out sites of strong points 1, 2, and 4 by day and to commence work on them with small parties. The size of the party is left to the discretion of the reconnoitring officer. The digging and wiring may be completed at night.
   Points 3 and 5 can only be approached by night and will be pegged out and sited at dusk if the tactical situation permits.

6. An order has been issued by the 18th Division that these parties will not be sent forward till IRLES is completely in our hands and the G.O.C., 53rd Infantry Brigade will be responsible for informing Os.C., Companies when the tactical situation permits of their being sent forward, and for the adequate covering of the parties at work.

7. Arrangements must be made for a reconnaissance of the best routes of approach to these points beforehand. This can be easily done from some of the high ground in our possession and Officers and senior N.C.Os must clearly know what they are going to do. The village of IRLES will not be entered by the strong point parties.

Page 2. ORDER N...

8. It must be impressed on all ranks that the early co... of these points is of the utmost importance in view of ... counter-attacks and that they must work 'all out' to co... them.

9. The completion of these points will be reported to the G.O.C. 53rd Brigade and to the C.R.E.

10. Strong points are allotted as follows :-

    79th Field Company, R.E. 1,2,3 and 4.
    92nd Field Company, R.E. 5.

11. It may be found necessary to improve these positions the following day. Immediate report should be made to the C.R.E as to this.

12. The 92nd Field Company R.E., less one* sections² will not work on "Z" day but will be ready to go to any locality for work at 15 minutes notice.

13. Companies will be located on "Z" day as follows :-

    79th Field Co.R.E. - 2 sections, 2 platoons MIRAUMONT.
                        2 sections, 2 platoons GRANDCOURT.
    92nd Field Co.R.E. - 1 section, 1 platoon MIRAUMONT.

14. ACKNOWLEDGE.

[signature]
Lieut R.E.
Acting Adjutant, 18th Divisional Engineers.

Issued at 6/30.am.9/3/17.

    Distribution :-

1. 79th Field Coy.R.E.
2. 92nd Field Coy.R.E.
3. 53rd Infantry Brigade.
4. War Diary.
5. File.

Army Form C. 2118

18th Divl R.E.
April 1917

Vol 19

WAR DIARY
or
INTELLIGENCE SUMMARY
(Erase heading not required.)

Place	Date	Hour	Summary of Events and Information	Remarks and references to Appendices
			During the month of April from 1st to 25th the CRE and Hd Qrs of Steenbecque with Division Hd Qrs, the Division being at rest. The Companies here occupied with training scheme and were inspected by the CE, II Corps on 16th and by the GOC 18th Div on 22nd. On 24th the 79th Coy marched to Bulls Green and was attached to the First Corps for work on the Writing. On 25th the 92nd Coy here moved to the ADLR Canadian Corps and worked till 28th when they returned to the Division at Beauquesne. During the last 3 days of the month the Companies here taken over from the respective Coys in the other division.	64

Shapes Lt RE
Adj 18th Divn RE

9/5/17

WAR DIARY
INTELLIGENCE SUMMARY

Headquarters 19th Division (Infantry).

MAY, 1917.

Army Form C. 2118

HQ Rs 185 Jof 25 20

Place	Date	Hour	Summary of Events and Information	Remarks and references to Appendices
Bouleux Wd Mauc.	9/5/17		On the front day of the work the Infantry moved out their guns and took over trenches from the out[?] and preparation for the attack in Chain trench immediately started and the new trenches and emplacements for the dumps for consolidation materials. Owing to the short notice at hand the divisions had just to the attack they were some difficulty in getting up the necessary stores for the dumps at the advanced Dump in general. As incessant shelling by the Germans to the later part of the previous Dumps to the extent of destroying the stores time and the fact rendered more difficult the replenishing of the regiment. On the 3rd the day of the attack the troops could not carry out their plans owing to the nature of the trenches and from the enemy was made to the new attack that there did not materialise and the reports to Corps carry. Short after the new plan the plan was a definite new plan and with that the Corps have seen ahead in effect such tactics. The left of the 14th Division on the left any of the matting the land and the regiment the left had S.P. was headed on a then on the head quarters of the Division boundary. On the 17th there have indication of retired withdrawal the enemy and in accordance with plan of the General Staff to deal with this retirement, the	65

WAR DIARY
or
INTELLIGENCE SUMMARY

MAY, 1917. Headquarters 14th Div. Engineers.

Page 2. Army Form C. 2118

66

Various strong point defensive positions bombing stops etc were arranged and allotted to the tps. on the lines of the three objectives and arrangements were made for reconnaissance of the whole sub-sector to the area captured in the advance.

This with drawel the enemy did not take place and the last part of the March was used to reinforce the trenches, push forward the front line & advance the sap and form up.

Dug out accommodation was improved and the defense lines were lined. Communication trenches were dug to the front line in the approach to the trenches were swept by M.G. fire.

One officer was wounded and several casualties occurred to the men and Vaillant platoons quartered in the neighbourhood of Hamel.

The H.Q. Dn. Hrs. between Beaurains and Scarfe, Villers St Lee when they moved to Basseux St Marc.

Hayes Lt Col
Adj 18th Div R.E.

WAR DIARY
or
INTELLIGENCE SUMMARY
(Erase heading not required.)

Army Form C. 2118

C.R.E. 18th Divn.
June 1917.

Vol 21

Place	Date	Hour	Summary of Events and Information	Remarks and references to Appendices
Nieuport	8th		From 1st June to 10th the Division H.Q. was at Bourlon. On Wed. and we relieved by the 58th Division, who took over schemes which were left uncompleted. H.Q. On removed to Coxin and the Field Companies were billeted at Sanselin, Gosnem & Sanslempré. On the 21st the Head Quarters and Field Companies entrained and went north and were transferred to the 11th Corps 5th Army and to the rest of the month worked to the 32nd Division. During this army the months were light considering that the companies were being in a frequently shelled area. Major Hayman 8.50 O.C. [?] Co. R.E. was wounded in action on the 14th.	67

Thayer, LtCol
Adjutant 18th Divn R.E.
R.E.O.

HEADQUARTERS 18TH DIVISIONAL ENGINEERS WAR DIARY FOR JULY 1917

Intelligence Summary

C.R.E., 18th DIVISION.

Army Form C. 2118

Place	Date	Hour	Summary of Events and Information	Remarks and references to Appendices
Eecke	6/7/17		From 1st to 7th July CRE and HQ Co. were at Hondeghem. Went to the 8th Division. The 30th Div. and 1st Bgde. respected 18th Div Hd Qrs. Co. 2/3 of the first were at Caëstre. Near Dunkerque. 1st was moving for the 30th Bn. R.E. of Hennekpt and the Companies that the Company of the 30th Bn. preparing to be ahead to the 31st Div. were stated at Ocre and a forward dump of R.E. Stores was ordered and filled. The greatest difficulty in the forward area has been lives of communication to the forward area. The light railway map was found unofficial and the Roads to Caestre were meagre. The second day and the Ypres Vanpour had to be used to dump stores to the towards Ypres. A Rly R.E. dump at Hondstedt had to be devoted by the 30th Division for that and in an easy drive to an Ypres. The officials of an division work to be preparations for attack of another division being the utmost than the light movement and business attention is required. Jan Hand dr. shows in the 31st Div hoped as he could be by and the but work day't do books what more of direction of the Ground in we engaged.	68

APPENDICES = "A.9.B." INSTRUCTIONS OF THE C.R.E. 18TH DIVISION TO ROYAL ENGINEERS AND PIONEERS, RESPECTIVELY.

J. Miles Lt. Col. R.E.
18th Division

SECRET   C.R.E. 18th Division
                                                       14/4/14.

INSTRUCTIONS TO ROYAL ENGINEERS FOR FORTHCOMING OPERATIONS

1. The 79th & 80th Field Companies will be allotted to the 53rd and 54th Infantry Brigades respectively for special work in connection with making the posts "A", "B", "C", "D", "E", "F", "G" and "H" on operation map and forming part of the garrison of the posts until relieved by orders from the Division.

   The 92nd Field Company will be in Divisional Reserve.

Assembly.

The 79th Field Company and attached platoons will be concentrated on "Y/Z" night with the remainder of the garrisons for the various posts, "A" to "D", and "1" to "12", in dug-outs in the West Bund of ZILLIBEKE LAKE, and in the RAILWAY Dug-outs, as ordered by the 53rd Infantry Brigade.

The 80th & 92nd Field Companies will be in Camp at H.26.b.5.6.

2. Operations.

The O.C.79th Field Co.R.E will be in touch with the 53rd Infantry Brigade, and as soon as the situation permits, the garrisons of the posts "A", "B", "C", "D" and Nos. 1,2,3,4,5,6,7,8,9,10,11 and 12 will move up as ordered : pick up stores and tools at the A.T.N. R.E.Dump in ZILLIBEKE and move forward independently to the various posts and commence work as soon as possible.

3. The O.C.80th Field Co.R.E will move into the CHATEAU SEGARD Area in time to start from there at ZERO plus 4 hours.

   The garrisons for posts "E", "F", "G" "H" and Nos. 13 to 36 will be formed into separate groups and move forward as soon as the situation permits, under orders of the 54th Infantry Brigade and pick up tools and stores at the A.T.N. R.E.Dump in ZILLIBEKE.

   A halt should be arranged for, and dinners or teas cooked in the RITZ Trench Area, and they should then proceed to their various posts according to the map issued.

   Route to RITZ STREET via A.T.N. Pack Track to ZILLIBEKE and subsequently by new track to be made and marked with tape and pickets.

4. Should an R.E.Officer be the Senior Officer in the garrison of a Post, he will be in command of the post and must clearly understand that under no circumstances must he retire or leave the post until ordered by the General Officer Commanding, 18th Division.

SECRET

Page 2.

5. R.E. Stores.

These will be obtained at the A.T.N. R.E. Dump, ZILLIBEKE, where they will be made up in "Man loads" and "pack loads" and arranged in heaps for each separate post "A" to "H" and Nos. "1" to "36".

It will be impossible to carry up all the necessary stores at once as the distances are great.

"Man loads" will be small.

Lists of extra stores required will be sent to the O.i/c ZILLIBEKE Dump, who will send them up by pack train, which will be sent up as soon as possible towards the evening. 20 pack animals will be allotted to the garrisons of posts "A", "B", "C", "D" and Nos. "1" to "12". 30 pack animals to posts "E", "F", "G", "H" and Nos. "13" to "36".

There are probably German Dumps of Pioneer Stores at J.15.c.55.50 and J.14.a.30.35, which should be utilised as far as possible.

When the demands of the various posts have been met it is hoped to start a more forward dump at a place to be notified later.

6. The O.C. 92nd Field Co. R.E will detail a small party under an officer to make a reconnaissance for water and send a report as soon as possible with samples for testing. They should be able to move forward when the 79th Field Company does.

7. The three Field Companies will at once prepare frames to enable R.E. Stores and tools to be carried on the ordinary saddle for 20 animals each.

8. Officers Commanding 79th & 80th Field Companies will have stores and tools made up into "Man loads" sufficient for the Posts to be furnished by their Brigades as soon as possible.

9. O.C. 92nd Field Company will provide 20 men including some R.E for work at the ZILLIBEKE Dump on "Z" Day.
They will await orders from the C.R.E before proceeding to ZILLIBEKE from their Camp on "Y/Z" night.

10. Information as to the progress of events can be obtained from Advanced Divisional Headquarters at H.27.b.5.7 from CHATEAU SEGARD, and from BEDFORD HOUSE.

PLEASE ACKNOWLEDGE.

C B O Symons

H.Q.R.E. 18th Division.
17 July, 1917.

Lieut. Colonel. R.E.
C.R.E. 18th Division.

Copies to :—
No. 1. "G" 18th Division.   No. 9. Div. Train.
No. 2. "Q" 18th Division.   No. 10. C.E. II Corps.
No. 3. 53rd Infantry Brigade.   No. 11. File.
No. 4. 54th Infantry Brigade.   No. 12. War Diary.
No. 5. 55th Infantry Brigade.
No. 6. 79th Field Coy. R.E.
No. 7. 80th Field Coy. R.E.
No. 8. 92nd Field Coy. R.E.

Distribution :-

Copy No. 1. 18th Division "G".
2. 18th Division A/Q.
3. 8th Royal Sussex Pioneers.
4. 53rd Infantry Brigade.
5. 55th Infantry Brigade.
6. 8th East Surrey Regt.
7. C.E. III Corps.
8. File.
9. War Diary. ✓
10. O.C. 18th Div Train.

Copy No 9.
B.
71

SECRET

C.R.E. 18th Division,
14/4/18.

INSTRUCTIONS FOR THE 8TH ROYAL SUSSEX PIONEERS AND THE BATTALION OF THE 55TH BRIGADE ALLOTTED TO C.R.E FOR WORK ON Z DAY

Disposition "Y/Z" night.

Advanced Headquarters, in touch with the Brigadier General, Commanding 53rd Infantry Brigade, in shelters in RIDGE STREET.
One platoon in the South end of RITZ STREET between VINCE and ZILLIBEKE STREETS. This platoon will be for marking out and reconnoitring the proposed track and will have an additional officer attached.
One Company in the Bund West of ZILLIBEKE LAKE.
Three Companies less one platoon in the CHATEAU SEGARD Area.
Should the Company undergoing instruction in Railway Construction be still detached, there will be only two companies less one platoon.
The 8th East Surrey Regiment will be in the CHATEAU SEGARD Area.

Work.

Three Companies of the 8th East Surrey Regiment will work with the corresponding Companies of the 8th Royal Sussex Regiment and will move forward when they do, under the orders of the Officer Commanding, 8th Royal Sussex Pioneers.
The fourth will be for special work as detailed below on the Tank Track.

A Mule Track will be made approximately as indicated on the plan issued to 8th Royal Sussex Regiment, and also a party will follow up in the wake of the Tanks and make their track passable for Field Artillery.
As soon as possible after ZERO, the RITZ trench platoon will go out with tape, pickets, etc., to mark out as much of the track as possible.
Work will commence as soon as practicable by the Company in ZILLIBEKE BUND, and its attached infantry company, which will be at CHATEAU SEGARD ready to move off as orders are received from the Officer Commanding, 8th Royal Sussex Pioneers, who will provide guides.
The other Companies will come up in sequence and go out on the work as the attack progresses.

Pack Track.- The track will be marked out as a preliminary measure with small pickets painted white, marked "A.T.N." in black letters, and tape : as time allows these will be substituted by heavier pickets and notice boards "A.T.N MULE TRACK".
Tank Track - One platoon of the 8th Royal Sussex Pioneers with the fourth company of Infantry will leave CHATEAU SEGARD at ZERO plus four hours and will follow the tanks from YEOMANRY POST and make the track good for Field Artillery Guns.
Stores. - All stores and tools will be collected at the A.T.N Pioneer Dump at I.22.b 8.4 near ZILLIBEKE and each Company will have their carrying parties detailed.

PLEASE ACKNOWLEDGE.

C B O Symons
Lieut Colonel, R.E
C.R.E. 18th Division.

H.Q.R.E. 18th Division.
17th July, 1917.

DISPOSITION OF R.E AND PIONEER UNITS ON "Z" DAY

UNIT.	Place of Assembly "Y/Z" Night.	Employment.	Work to be done.	Remarks.
9th Field Co. R.E and attached platoons	ZILLEBEKE LAKE West End.	Consolidation.	Making and garrisoning of Strong Points "A", "B", "C" and "D".	One platoon of Infantry and one R.E.Detachment will form part of the garrison of each post and be available for work.
10th Field Co. R.E and attached platoons	H.26.b.5.5.	-do-	Making and garrisoning of Strong Points "E", "F", "G" and "H".	-do-
2nd Field Co. R.E.	H.26.b.5.6.	Divisional Reserve.	One small party on water reconnaissance under an officer. Loading party at R.E.Dump, ZILLEBEKE.	
8th Royal Sussex Regt (Pioneers).	One platoon S. end of RITZ St. One Coy W. end of ZILLEBEKE LAKE. = 3 Coys. less 1 platoon CHATEAU SEGARD Area.	Communications.	(i) Making pack track - 3 Coys less 1 platoon. (ii)Tank Track - improving for R.F.A. (1 platoon). One Coy - Light Railways under A.D.L.R if required, otherwise on pack track.	* If Company under Railway Construction returns.
5th East Surrey Regt.	CHATEAU SEGARD Area.	Communications.	3 Coys on Pack Track. 1 Coy on Tank Track.	Coys will work with corresponding Companies of 8th R.Sussex Pioneers.

WAR DIARY
or
INTELLIGENCE SUMMARY

Army Form C. 2118

R.E. 18th Divn.

Vol 24

Place	Date	Hour	Summary of Events and Information	Remarks and references to Appendices
Caguelbeeg	Sept 1917 23rd		Field Companies & K1 areas training etc in proper.	74
Poperinghe	24th		H.Q. Divisional Engineers moved from Caguelbeeg area and took up billets of N.Z. Division H.Q. Cm RE.	
	29th		On 29th Sept. the three Field Coys were brought up in busses and prepared camp for themselves	

Thaper Capt RE.
Adjutant 18th D. RE.

AO R5187
10/25

75

WAR DIARY or INTELLIGENCE SUMMARY

Army Form C. 2118

(Erase heading not required.)

Place	Date	Hour	Summary of Events and Information	Remarks and references to Appendices
ELVERDINGHE	10.11.17		For the first three days of October CHQ and Headquarters were in POPERINGHE. On Oct. 4th the 11th & 16th went to City Mond & Advanced DHQ to Canal Bank. Adjutant remained at BORDER CAMP. The Division relieved the 11th Division and maintained two Headquarters for the remainder of the month till 25th when it was relieved by the 58th Division. Field Sections were employed in forward communications and forward camps. The 79th Fd Co took part in the attack on POELCAPELLE on 22nd. Casualties during the month were very light.	

Nasha Capt RE
Adjutant 18th Div RE

10.11.17

===========
S E C R E T
===========

C.R.E. 18th Div No./9/3/65.

Headquarters.
  18th Division. A.

Herewith War Diaries for the 18th Divisional Engineers for the month of November 1917.

9th December 1917.

for, C.R.E. 18th Division.
Captain R.E.

WAR DIARY
INTELLIGENCE SUMMARY

Place: ELVERDINGHE
Date: 9/11/17

From Novr 1st - Novr 3rd the Division was out of the line. On the 4th the Division relieved the 35th Division and on the 11th a portion of the 50th Division front was taken over Division of On moved to ELVERDINGHE. Owing to the change of Corps at the same time as that of the Division the demand for R.E. reinforcement was very great and difficult. Her experience in meeting requirement of the three Corps were working in forward area claimed the whole month, as a front line work and has in communication and general work. As the Somme fighting had been a test to late date, the weather became bad before men had had had a chance to dine to avoid the bad effects of the trouble fell to the drawn off of their labour and food troops were most important work undertaken. A scheme has not accumulated in the mind during the month of troops in support. Scheme for troops in the Corps line. This is in process now and is being worked by the 173rd & 253rd Tunnelling Coy R.E.

77

Thafer Capt MRO
Aug 15 D.R.E.

78

WAR DIARY or INTELLIGENCE SUMMARY

Place: Oosthoek

Dec. 1st to 16th — Div HQrs R.E. at Oosthoek Chateau. Still
Coy in vicinity of Yser Canal. Main work consisted in
communications to front line and drainage of Inundations.
On 18th the Divisional HQrs relieved by 57th Division. I went
at once. CRE A/Cof CRSO Seymour DSO R.E. became CRE
Army line and M.T. Gn. moved to Oosthoeve Camp.
Reconnaissance of Army line was commenced and initial
preparation of defences + drainage were started.
On Jan 5th this work was handed on to Major Weber
a/CRE 1st Division.
On Jan 3rd R.E. 1st Gn. relieved 1st Chateau and Gels top.
& then signed camps 92nd Fld Coy RE went out the line.
79th & 60th Coys a communications + drainage.

Shafer left Pl
a/) 1st Div RE

WAR DIARY
INTELLIGENCE SUMMARY

Headquarters 18th Divr. R.E.

Vol 28

Army Form C. 2118

79

Place	Date	Hour	Summary of Events and Information	Remarks and references to Appendices
ELVERDINGHE	1-1-18		On Jan 31st the Division relieved the 57th Division in the line. O.C.E. & H.Q. Ox moved from CHARTERHOUSE CAMP & ELVERDINGHE CHATEAU. Jan 3rd. CRE handed over work in ARMY BATTLE ZONE to CRE 1st Division. 2nd & 3rd/1st Field Covy took on the same camps evacuated on Dec 18th. Two Companies were employed on Corps Defence Line and one will to-night in the line. Flood a 15th Place! commenced to extend line in a precarious condition and High Land Post being constructed over the Steen beek at U.21.d.0.3. The Division was relieved by 32nd Division on January 30th.	

Thatcher Capt RE
Adj 18th Divn RE

WAR DIARY or INTELLIGENCE SUMMARY

Army Form C. 2118

No 16 18th Div R.E.

Vol 29

Place	Date	Hour	Summary of Events and Information	Remarks and references to Appendices
ROUEZ	1/2/18		From Feb 10-7th the Division was out of the line - 111 Coy trained in the Rouez area. 8th, 9th & 10th Division to transferred L 3rd Army and moved by train to Noyon area. Division H.Q. at Salency. 13th CRR took over work of Corp. Battle zone. 111th Coy took over work a Corps Battle Zone in hand. South sector refecting Division relieved 58th Division on 27th. ORR & H.Q. at Rouez	80

Shufer Capt RE
A/g 'G' Div RE

SECRET. Copy. No.......

18TH DIVISION.

C. R. E.'s OPERATION ORDER. NO. 25.

Ref. Map Sheets.
66.c. & 70.d.
1/40.000.

Headquarters. R.E.
18th Division.

23rd February. 1918.

1. The 18th Division will relieve the Northern Brigade of 58th Division, and the Southern Brigade of 14th Division in the LIEZ and LY FONTAINE Sectors respectively, with boundaries as detailed in my No. 42/5. of the 22nd Instant.

2. The 92nd Field Co R.E. will take over the work at present being done by the 511th Field Co R.E. 58th Division, O.C. 92nd Co R.E. should meet O.C. 511th Co R.E. at 9.a.m. on the 24th Instant at MENNESSIS to take over.

3. The Company less 1 Section will take over the Billets and Horse lines of the 511th Co R.E. at MENNESSIS and RUEZ respectively on the 25th Instant. Move to be completed by 5.p.m.
   1 Section will remain at VENDEUIL as at present.

4. Work on the Centre and Right Sectors of the Right Division Battle Zone will be handed over as follows:-
   Centre Sector to O.C. 503rd Field Co R.E. at VIRY NOUREUIL on 25th Instant, time to be arranged between Company Commanders.
   Right Sector, Partly to O.C. 504th Field Co R.E. at BUTTE-de-RUEZ at 9.a.m. on the 24th Inst,
   Partly to an officer of the 511th Field Co R.E. who will be at the R.E. Dump PIERREMANDE at 9.a.m. on the 25th Instant.
   Indents for Working Parties for these two Sectors, up to, and including the 26th Inst will be sent in by O.C. 92nd Field Co R.E. to 58th Division.

5. The 79th Field Co R.E. will take over the work of the 89th Field Co R.E. 14th Division.
   O.C. 79th Field Co R.E. will arrange direct with O.C. 89th Field Co R.E. as to time and place.
   The Company less 1 Section will take over the Billets and Horse Lines of the 89th Field Co R.E. at REMIGNY.
   1 Section will be billeted at LY FONTAINE.
   Relief to be completed by 5.p.m. on the 26th Instant.

6. Work on the Centre, and Left Sectors of the 14th Division Battle Zone, will be handed over to Works Officers of the 14th Division at present acting as Liason Officers, on the 26th.
   The Section at work on the Southern Sector will continue to work in this Sector until further orders.

7. Orders for the move of the 80th Field Co R.E. will be issued later

8. C.R.E.'s Office will close at CHAUNY, and open at RUEZ on the 27th February.

9. Acknowledge.

Issued at: 9. p.m.

Lieut Colonel R.E.
Commanding Royal Engineer. 18th Division.

(Distribution over.)

Distribution:-

Copy No. 1. O.C. 79th Field Co R.E.
"   "   2. O.C. 80th Field Co R.E.
"   "   3. O.C. 92nd Field Co R.E.
"   "   4. C.R.E. 14th Division.
"   "   5. C.R.E. 58th Division.
"   "   6. 18th Division G.
"   "   7. 18th Division A/Q.
"   "   8. Chief Engineer. III Corps.
"   "   9. 53rd Inf Bde.
"   " 10. 54th Inf Bde.
"   " 11. 55th Inf Bde.
"   " 12. O.C. 18th Div Train. & S.S.O.
"   " 13. O.C. 18th Div Signals.
"   " 14. A.C. MENNESSIS.
"   " 15. A.C. RUEZ.
"   " 16. A.C. REMIGNY.
"   " 17. A.C. LY FONTAINE.
"   " 18. War Diary.
"   " 19. File.

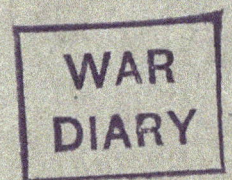

Headquarters,

ROYAL ENGINEERS, 18th Division.

M A R C H

1 9 1 8

Army Form C. 2118

WAR DIARY for MARCH, 1918.
or
INTELLIGENCE SUMMARY
Headquarters, 18th Divisional Engineers.

(Erase heading not required.)

Place	Date	Hour	Summary of Events and Information	Remarks and references to Appendices
ROUEZ. ST-QUENTIN Sheet.	March 1918 1st.	---	From 1st to 20th March, the Headquarters were at ROUEZ, and Companies were employed on the Corps Defensive Line, preparations for destruction of Bridges, in case a withdrawal was necessary. On the night of 20/21st as a German attack seemed likely, the order was received to "PREPARE FOR ATTACK", followed by:- "MAN BATTLE POSITIONS" at 5.40.a.m. The 79th, and 92nd Field Companies R.E. accordingly "STOOD TO" in the BATTLE ZONE, and the charges were placed in prepared places on the 8 Bridges over the CROZAT CANAL in the Divisional Area. The 80th Field Company R.E. assembled at MENNESSIS, and was found there by the Section which was detached, and working under the C.R.E. III Corps Troops. From the opening of the German attack on the morning of the 21st March 1918 to the night of 25th march, the Field Companies took part in rearguard actions, and assisted the Infantry when necessary 8 Bridges over the CROZAT CANAL were successfully destroyed, and one over the OISE CANAL. moves of Headquarters R.E. were as follows:- 21/22nd From ROUEZ to UGNY-Le-GAY. 23/24th From UGNY - Le - GAY, to BABOEUF. 24/25th BABOEUF to VARESNES. 25/26th VARESNES to CAIGNES, 26th, CAIGNES to AUDIGNICOURT. 29th, 30th & 31st the Divisional Engineers were taken by Busses to AMIENS Area. C.R.E., and Divisional Headquarters at BOVES.	

10th April, 1918.

[signature]
Captain R.E.
Adjutant R.E.
for, C.R.E. 18th Division.

82

SECRET.   Copy No. 15.

18TH DIVISION.

C.R.E's OPERATION ORDER. NO. 26.

Ref. Map Sheets.   Headquarters. R.E.
66.C. & 70.E.   18th Division.
1/40.000.
                                                        9th March. 1918.

1. The 80th Field Company R.E. (less one Section) will return to the 18th Division on the 10th March. 1918.

2. One Section will remain on the FLAVY – CLASTRES Road, until completion, when it will rejoin the 80th Field Co R.E.

3. (a) Headquarters, and Transport Lines, will be at ROUEZ.
    (b) One Section at MENNESSIS.
    (c) Two Sections at REMIGNY.

4. One lorry will report at 80th Field Co R.E. H.Q. at COMMENCHON at 7.a.m. on the 10th Instant, for the purpose of moving surplus stores etc.

    One lorry will report at 111 Corps R.E. Dump FLAVY at 9.a.m. with 4 Bell Tents, and will load with R.E. material, and proceed to REMIGNY. 80th Field Co R.E. will provide guide at FLAVY R.E. DUMP at 9.a.m. and will go through with lorry to destination.

5. Completion of move will be reported to this office by wire.

6. Acknowledge.

Issued at:-

                                                        Captain R.E.
                                                for, C.R.E. 18th Division.

Distribution:-

Copy No.	1.	O.C. 80th Field Co R.E.
"	2.	C.R.E. 111 Corps Troops.
"	3.	Chief Engineer, 111 Corps.
"	4.	O.C. 79th Field Co R.E.
"	5.	O.C. 92nd Field Co R.E.
"	6.	"G" 18th Division.
"	7.	"A/Q" 18th Division.
"	8.	53rd Inf Bde.
"	9.	54th Inf Bde.
"	10.	55th Inf Bde.
"	11.	O.C. 18th Div'l Train. & S.S.O.
"	12.	O.C. 18th Div'l Signals.
"	13.	A.C. VILLEQUIER AUMONT.
"	14.	A.C. REMIGNY.
"	15.	War Diary.
"	16.	Office.

Headquarters,

ROYAL ENGINEERS, 18th Division.

A P R I L

1 9 1 8

WAR DIARY
or
INTELLIGENCE SUMMARY

Army Form C. 2118

WO R8/18D

April 1931

Place	Date	Hour	Summary of Events and Information	Remarks and references to Appendices
CAVILLON. Ref. AMIENS Sheet. 1/100.000.	1st.		From April 1st to 13th, C.R.E.'s Headquarters were at BOVES with Headquarters of the Division. The Field Companies were engaged on the Defences in the neighbourhood of, GENTELLES and VILLERS BRETONNEUX. and Support Lines. On the 13th The 58th Division took over, and the Division moved into support. C.R.E.'s. H.Q. moved to ST FUSCIEN, On the 26th the Division moved back into the Rest Area at CAVILLON. The Field Companies were engaged in improving billet accommodation in their Brigade Areas, and training. The Division was still out of the Line on the 30th. 9th May 1918.	85

Captain R.E.
Adjutant R.E.
for, C.R.E. 18th Division.

Army Form C. 2118

WAR DIARY
or
INTELLIGENCE SUMMARY
(Erase heading not required.)

18th Durh. R.
May 1918.

Place	Date	Hour	Summary of Events and Information	Remarks and references to Appendices

From May 1st 5th Divisional HQ RE were at CAVILLON. A 5th RE mess
at BAVELINCOURT. The 6th, 74th, 56th field Coys worked with the 47 Division
the 91st Coy were along in the sectors and had taken and worked the
5th Australian Fld Coy & May 1st. Companies been employed in accommodation
and defense works in the Flying Corps fields till 23rd when the Division
moved into Corps reserve and took in improvement Defenses / WARLOY
and BAIZIEUX LINES. weather during the month of May was very light

Major [signature]
Ag 18 Div RE

7.6.18.

86

Army Form C. 2118

WAR DIARY
or
INTELLIGENCE SUMMARY
HQ 18th Div R.E.

(Erase heading not required.)

Instructions regarding War Diaries and Intelligence Summaries are contained in F.S. Regs., Part II. and the Staff Manual respectively. Title Pages will be prepared in manuscript.

Place	Date	Hour	Summary of Events and Information	Remarks and references to Appendices
CONTAY. Sheet. 57/D.	June ~~JULY.~~ 9th. 1918.		On the 11th June, C.R.E. and Headquarters, moved to Shelters at S.W. end of VADENCOURT WOOD. The Field Companies R.E. were employed during the month on improvements in the forward trenches, including wiring, erecting Company, and Platoon H.Qs., Making Strong Points, etc. A considerable amount of work was devoted to making Divisional Headquarters, Brigade Headquarters, and the Divisional Training Camp at MOLLIENS-AU-BOIS. On the 27th June, the WARLOY SECTOR, of the BAIZIEUX DEFENCE SYSTEM was manned, this being the line which would be held by the Field Companies R.E. and other R.E. units, in the event of an attack. During the month casualties were very light. APPENDICES ATTACHED. 1. Nominal Roll of Officers, 18th Divisional Engineers, for month ending 29th June. 2. C.R.E.'s. Operation Order No. 131. dated 12th June. 3. C.R.E.'s. Operation Order No. 132. dated 26th June. 4. C.R.E.'s. Letter No. 27/3. (Attached to Order No. 132.)	

Captain R.E.
for, Lieut Colonel R.E.
Commanding Royal Engineer, 18th Division.

C.R.E. 18th Div No. 45/44.

Nominal Roll of Officers.
18th Divisional Engineers.

89.

Rank, and Name.		Status.	Unit.	Date of 1st Commission.
Bvt/Lieut Col. C.B.O. Symons. (D.S.O.)		Reg.	C. R. E.	19. 10. 94.
A/Major R.E. Knight.	(M.C.)	S.R.	O.C. 79th Field Coy R.E.	24. 10. 14.
A/Captain G.P. Geen.	(M.C.)	T.C.	" " "	5. 6. 16.
T/Lieut D.A. Mackay.		T.C.	" " "	9. 6. 15.
T/2nd Lieut G.A. Young.		T.F.	" " "	1. 4. 17.
T/2nd Lieut A.R. Haynes.		T.F.	" " "	1. 4. 17.
T/2nd Lieut R.J. Reed.		T.F.	" " "	19. 8. 17.
T/2nd Lieut P.E. Knight.		T.C.	" " "	17. 11. 17.
A/Major G. Ledgard.	(M.C.)	T.C.	O.C. 80th Field Coy R.E.	25. 3. 15.
A/Captain R. Weir.	(M.C.)	T.C.	" " "	7. 5. 16.
T/Lieut A.J. Phillips.		T.C.	" " "	17. 11. 15.
T/2nd Lieut S. Hoare.		T.C.	" " "	28. 3. 17.
2nd Lieut N.D. Mackay.		REG.	" " "	15. 5. 17.
T/2nd Lieut A.C. James.		T.C.	" " "	28. 10. 17.
T/2nd Lieut A.H. Watson.		T.C.	" " "	28. 10. 17.
A/Major E.D. Alexander.	(M.C.)	T.C.	O.C. 92nd Field Coy R.E.	20. 8. 15.
T/Captain T.C.B. Davies.		T.F.	" " "	25. 2. 15.
T/Lieut H.J. Parham.		T.F.	" " "	8. 12. 14.
T/2nd Lieut J.R. Bayley.		T.C.	" " "	14. 7. 17.
T/2nd Lieut A.F. Hall.		T.C.	" " "	28. 10. 17.
T/2nd Lieut F.J. Meen.		T.C.	" " "	28. 10. 17.
T/2nd Lieut B. Wood.		T.C.	" " "	15. 12. 17.
T/2nd Lieut R.D. Alexander.		T.C.	" " "	12. 1. 18.

Casualties, and Changes during the Month.

Captain L. Napier. R.E. (S.R.) (Late Adjutant R.E.) 18th Division.	Transferred to 15th Field Coy R.E. and to Command that Unit. Authority. A.Gs. NO. A.G./55/2880. (O) Left 23/6/18.
T/2nd Lieut G. Harley. (M.C.) T.F.	Wounded in Action. 5/6/18.
T/2nd Lieut R.D. Alexander. T.C.	Joined 92nd Field Coy R.E. 18/6/18.
T/2nd Lieut F.J. Meen. T.C.	Joined 92nd Field Coy R.E. 20/6/18.

SD/. C.B.O. Symons

29th June 1918.

Lieut Colonel R.E.
Commanding Royal Engineer, 18th Division.

SECRET.   Copy No........

18TH DIVISION.

C. R. E.'s OPERATION ORDER NO. 131.

Reference Map Sheets.   Headquarters R.E.
No. 57/D. and 62/D.   18th Division.
    1/40,000.
                                                                   12th June, 1918.

1.   The 80th Field Company R.E. will relieve the 79th Field Company R.E. in the Left Brigade Sector, of the Divisional Front, on the 16th Instant.

2.   The details of relief will be arranged direct between Os. C. concerned.

3.   The 79th Field Company R.E. on relief, will not take over the work at MOLLIENS-AU-BOIS, at present being done by the 80th Coy R.E.

4.   Billets, and Transport Lines of each Company will remain as at present.

5.   Completion of relief will be notified to this Office.

6.   Acknowledge.

Issued. at.:-........

                                                                      Captain R.E.
                                                             for, C.R.E. 18th Division.

Distribution.

Copy No.		
" "	1.	O.C. 79th Field Coy R.E.
" "	2.	O.C. 80th Field Coy R.E.
" "	3.	O.C. 92nd Field Coy R.E.
" "	4.	18th Division G.
" "	5.	18th Division A/Q.
" "	6.	53rd Infantry Brigade.
" "	7.	54th Infantry Brigade.
" "	8.	55th Infantry Brigade.
" "	9.	O.C. 18th Div Signals.
" "	10.	War Diary.
" "	11.	File.

SECRET.   Copy No.........

18TH DIVISION.

C. R. E.'s OPERATION ORDER. NO. 132.

Reference Map   Headquarters. R.E.
Sheet. SMILLIS.   18th Division.
1/20.000.
                                                                 26th June 1918.

1. Reference 111 Corps Defence Scheme. Para 6.d.

    There will be a test manning of the BAIZIEUX SYSTEM - WARLOY SECTOR, on the 27th Instant, by the units mentioned below, in addition to the Field Companies R.E. of the 18th Division.

        1st Siege Company R.A., R.E.
        259th Army Troops Company R.E.
        253rd Tunnelling Coy R.E.

    These will be under the Command of the O.C. 1st Siege Coy, R.A. R.E., the whole under the Command of the C.R.E.

2. Units will take up positions accoding to the attached tracing, and as recently indicated to O.Cs. on the ground.

    N.B. Normally on the first indication of an impending attack, orders to "MAN BATTLE STATIONS" - ACKNOWLEDGE, will be sent to Units, but in this instance they will be manned at 8.a.m. on the 27th, without further orders.

3. The Headquarters of C.R.E. will be at V.25.c.2.9. in the small fir copse.

4. As soon as units are in position, a runner will be sent to C.R.E. reporting to that effect. This runner will remain at C.R.E.'s H.Q. at V.25.c.2.9. for duty.

5. VISUAL COMMUNICATIONS.

    The 92nd Field Coy R.E. (in reserve.) will send men trained in signalling, to C.R.E.'s H.Q. Other Company Commanders who have trained signallers will establish visual signalling stations between their H.Q. and C.R.E.'s H.Q.

6. In this instance, only haversack rations will be taken, water bottles full, but a scheme will be prepared, and skeleton arrangements made for cooking, and supplies of ammunition, water, etc, as if for a long occupation of the line.

    A certain number of tools for consolidation purposes, and tools for cutting purposes should also be taken.

7. DRESS.   Fighting Order.

8. MEDICAL ARRANGEMENTS.

    The M.O. R.E. 18th Division will establish R.A.P. about V.25. and the M.O. 253rd Tunnelling Coy R.E., R.A.P. in vicinity of D.1.a.0.0.

    Wounded should be sent to 56th Field Ambulance, WARLOY, U.24.c.5.7.

    56th Field Ambulance are in charge of the evacuation of the forward area.

                                                                    P.T.O.

8. **MEDICAL ARRANGEMENTS. (continued.)**

55th Field Ambulance are in charge of the Main Dressing Station, VADENCOURT.

9. Please acknowledge.

Issued at...........

                  Lieut Colonel R.E.
               C.R.E. 18th Division.

Distribution.

Copy No.	1.	O.C. 79th Field Coy R.E.
"	2.	O.C. 80th Field Coy R.E.
"	3.	O.C. 92nd Field Coy R.E.
"	4.	O.C. 1st Siege Coy R.A, R.E.
"	5.	O.C. 239th Army Troops Coy R.E.
"	6.	O.C. 253rd Tunnelling Coy R.E.
"	7.	18th Division "G".
"	8.	War Diary.
"	9.	File.

SECRET. C.R.E. 18th Div No. 27/3.

92

War Diary.

Reference my order No. 132. (attached.)

(a) As soon as men are in position, each man should be definitely told off to a fire position.
Ranges to prominent objects should be taken, and range cards made.

(b) Units, Machine Guns, Lewis Guns, and H.Q. on both flanks, and in vicinity, should be known by all, and any dead ground in front.
It is the duty of the unit on the left to keep in liason with the next unit on its right.

(c) Trenches made fightable, Latrines made, and field of fire cleared, and positions for 3 Lewis Guns per Company made.

(d) Section Commanders should practice manning trenches, and giving a few words of command, and control of fire.

It is almost certain that the G.O.C. 18th Division, with certain Officers, and N.C.O.'s of the American Army will be inspecting the line about 10.a.m.

O.C. Sections of Defence, should have a scheme of work prepared, showing, what they would do, had they to hold the line for some time.

N.B. Company Commanders will meet me at my H.Q. at V.25.c.2.9. at 9.30.a.m. on the 27th.

26th June 1918.
Lieut Colonel R.E.
Commanding Royal Engineer, 18th Division.

Addressed to all recipients of Order No. 132.

Army Form C. 2118.

WAR DIARY
or
INTELLIGENCE SUMMARY

(Erase heading not required.)

HQ RE 18D Vol 34

93

Place	Date	Hour	Summary of Events and Information	Remarks and references to Appendices
	July '18			
	AUGUST.			
ST.GRATIEN. Sheet. 62.D.	10th 19 18.		On July 8/9th there was a test manning of Battle Stations by night, the Field Companies occupying part of the WARLOY SECTOR of the BAIZIEUX SYSTEM.	
			On July 11th the 79th and 80th Field Companies were relieved by units of the 47th Division. The 92nd Field Company was relieved on July 12th. C.R.E's H.Q. moved to PICQUIGNY (Sheet 62.E.) on the 13th and the Division came into G.H.Q. Reserve. Whilst in G.H.Q. Reserve Field Companies carried out Training Programmes.	
			On July 30th, 80th Field Company R.E., and on July 31st, 92nd Field Company R.E. took over work from units of 5th Australian Division.	
			APPENDICES ATTACHED.
-*-*-*-*-*-*-*-*-	
			1. Nominal Roll of Officers, 18th Divisional Engineers, for Month of JULY.	
			2. C.R.E's OPERATION ORDER No.133. dated 28th July 1918.	
			-*-*-=-*-=-*-=-*-	
			[signature] Captain R.E.
for, Lieut Colonel R.E.
Commanding Royal Engineers 18th Division.	

Nominal Roll of Officers. — 18th Divisional Engineers.

Rank. Substantive. and Acting.	Name.	Status.	Unit.	Date of Commission.	Date of Present Rank.
Major. Bvt/Lieut.Colonel.	C.B.O. Symons. D.S.O.	Reg.	C.R.E. 18th Division.	19. 10. 94.	19. 3. 17.
T/Lieut. A/Captain.	G.H. Kohl.	T.C.	Adjutant.	28. 8. 15.	14. 12. 17.
Captain. A/Major.	K.I. Gourlay. M.C.	Reg.	O.C. 79th Field Coy R.E.	26. 7. 11.	10. 7. 18.
T/Lieut. A/Captain.	G.P. Geen. M.C.	T.C.	"	3. 6. 16.	26. 5. 18.
T/Lieutenant.	D.A. Mackay.	T.C.	"	6. 6. 15.	17. 11. 17.
T/2nd Lieutenant.	G.A. Young.	T.F.	"	1. 4. 17.	
T/2nd Lieutenant.	A.R. Haynes.	T.F.	"	1. 4. 17.	
T/2nd Lieutenant.	R.J. Reed.	T.F.	"	19. 8. 17.	
T/2nd Lieutenant.	P.E. Knight.	T.C.	"	17. 11. 17.	
T/Captain. A/Major.	G. Ledgard. M.C.	T.C.	O.C. 80th Field Coy R.E.	25. 3. 15.	24. 3. 18.
T/Lieut. A/Captain.	R. Weir. M.C.	T.C.	"	7. 5. 16.	24. 3. 18.
T/Lieutenant.	A.J. Phillips.	T.C.	"	17. 11. 15.	1. 7. 17.
T/2nd Lieutenant.	S. Hoare.	T.C.	"	28. 3. 17.	
2nd Lieutenant.	N.D. Mackay.	Reg.	"	15. 5. 17.	
T/2nd Lieutenant.	A.C. James.	T.C.	"	28. 10. 17.	
T/2nd Lieutenant.	A.H. Watson.	T.C.	"	28. 10. 17.	
T/Captain. A/Major.	E.D. Alexander. M.C.	T.C.	O.C. 92nd Field Coy R.E.	20. 8. 15.	7. 3. 18.
T/Lieutenant.A/Captain.	T.C.B. Davies.	T.F.	"	25. 2. 15.	14. 4. 16.
T/Lieutenant.	H.J. Parham.	T.F.	"	9. 12. 14.	1. 6. 16.
T/2nd Lieutenant.	J.R. Bayley.	T.C.	"	14. 7. 17.	
T/2nd Lieutenant.	A.F. Hall.	T.C.	"	28. 10. 17.	
T/2nd Lieutenant.	F.J. Meen.	T.C.	"	28. 10. 17.	
T/2nd Lieutenant.	B. Wood.	T.C.	"	15. 12. 17.	
T/2nd Lieutenant.	R.D. Alexander.	T.C.	"	12. 1. 18.	

P. T. O.

CASUALTIES AND CHANGES DURING THE MONTH OF JULY.

Lieut. A/Captain. G.H. Kohl. R.E., T.C. Joined from R.E. Base Depot. Appointed Adjutant R.E. 18th Division, vice Captain L. Napier R.E., S.R. Transferred. Date of Appointment. 7/7/18.

Captain. A/Major. K.I. Gourlay. R.E., Reg. Joined from R.E. Base Depot. Appointed to Command 79th Field (M.G.) Coy R.E., vice Captain A. Major R.E. Knight M.C. R.E., S.R. Transferred to R.E. Base Depot. Date of Appointment. 19/7/18.

SECRET.   Copy No........

18th DIVISION.

C.R.E.'s OPERATION ORDER. No. 133.

Reference Map Sheets.   Headquarters. R.E.
    62./D. 1/40,000.   18th Division.

                                                        28th July. 1918.

1. Relief of R.E. 5th Australian Division by R.E. of 18th Division.

2. The 18th Division will relieve the 5th Australian Division in the line on July 31st 1918.
    The 54th, and 55th Infantry Brigades will be in the line, with the 54th Brigade on the Right.
    53rd Infantry Brigade will be in Reserve.

3. Field Companies R.E. will move by Bus in accordance with attached table.

4. Transport will proceed by road.

5. The 79th Field Coy will load up all Pontoons and Gear, and send it to VILLERS BOCAGE on 31st, where it will be dumped, the party will stage the night 31/1st at VILLERS BOCAGE, reporting to C.R.E. III Corps Troops on arrival.
    An Officer of the 79th Field Coy R.E. will be in charge of the party.
    Two O.R. of 79th Fd Coy R.E. will remain at VILLERS BOCAGE in charge of the Pontoons.
    They will be rationed, and billeted from August 1st by C.R.E. III Corps Troops.

6. C.R.E.'s. Office will close at PICQUIGNY on the morning of August 1st, and will re-open at ST-GRATIEN the same day.

7. Please acknowledge.

Issued at-:...........   Captain R.E.
                                                        for, C.R.E. 18th Division.

            Distribution.

            Copy No. 1. C.R.E. 5th Australian Division.
              "   " 2. O.C. 79th Field Coy R.E.
              "   " 3. O.C. 80th Field Coy R.E.
              "   " 4. O.C. 92nd Field Coy R.E.
              "   " 5. War Diary.
              "   " 6. Office.

P.T.O.

MOVE TABLE to Accompany C.R.E.'s ORDER No. 133.

Serial No.	Unit.	Unit to be relieved.	Date.	From.	To.	Embus at.	Debus at.	Remarks.
1.	80th Fd Co. R.E.	14th Fd Co. A.E.	29/7/18.	LA-CHAUSSEE.	I.6.c.5.7 - Transport C.27 Cent.	11 A.M.	LA-HOUSSOYE	Embussing Pt. Church at LA-CHAUSSEE.
	Advance party 92rd Fd Co R.E.		29/7/18.	do.		11.a.m.	do.	do.
2.	92nd Fd Co. R.E.	15th Fd Co. A.E.	30/7/18.	do.	I.28.b.1.9. Transport H.5.d.2.7.	11.a.m.	do.	do.
	Advance party 79th Fd. Co. R.E.		do.	do.		11.a.m.	do.	do.
3.	79th Fd Co. R.E.	8th Fd Co. A.E.	31/7/18.	do.	I.5.a.2.2. Transport C.28.d.7.5.	12 noon.	do.	do.

18th DIVISION.

C. R. E.

18th DIVISION

AUGUST 1918

Army Form C. 2118.

WAR DIARY
or
INTELLIGENCE SUMMARY

(Erase heading not required.)

HQ R.E. 18D Vol 35

August 1916

97

Place	Date	Hour	Summary of Events and Information	Remarks and references to Appendices
ST.GRATIEN. Sheet 62.D.	Aug. 1st to 6th.		C.R.E.'s H.Q. moved to ST.GRATIEN on August 1st. Field Companies working on Battle Headquarters, preparing Wiring Material Etc.	
	" 7th.		C.R.E.'s advanced H.Q. in HEILLY.	
	" 8th. " 9th.		Field Companies digging Strong Points and consolidating line gained in attack along BRAY - CORBIE Road.	
	" 10th.		Field Companies moved after dark to 47th Division Area.	
	" 11th.		Field Companies relieved Field Companies of 47th Division. 79th Fd.Coy. in Centre Sector, 80th Fd. Coy in Left Sector, 92nd Field Coy. in Reserve. Right Sector held by 129th Regt.U.S.N.G.	
CONTAY. Sheet 57.D.	" 12th		C.R.E.'s H.Q. moved to CONTAY.	
	" 13th to 21st.		Field Companies working on Shelters, harvesting Wheat, repairing roads and tracks. Also preparing 20 Portable Footbridges 24' to 30' Span for passage of R.ANCRE.	
	" 22nd.		Division attacked over the ANCRE RIVER. 80th and 92nd Field Companies put 12 Footbridges across R.ANCRE at ZERO and 6 WELDON TRESTLE Bridges over ANCRE River during the day. 79th Field Coy standing by with advanced guard.	
HENENCOURT. Sheet 57.D.	" 24th.		C.R.E.'s H.Q. moved to HENENCOURT.	
	" 25th.		C.R.E.'s advanced H.Q. at BECOURT CHATEAU.	
	" 26th to 31st.		Companies working on Water Supply in forward Area as advance continued and making Dry Weather Tracks. C.R.E.'s H.Q. moved to BECOURT CHATEAU on 29th Inst and to S.27.a.2.8. CATERPILLAR VALLEY (Sheet 57.C.) on 31st.	

P.T.O.
****

Captain.R.E.
for Major.R.E.
A/C.R.E. 18th Division.

APPENDICES ATTACHED.

1. Nominal Roll of Officers, 18th Divisional Engineers, for Month of August.

2. C.R.E's OPERATION ORDER No. 136. dated 20th August 1918.

3. Total Casualties in Field Companies R.E. 18th Div. during August.

Nominal Roll of Officers --- 18th Divisional Engineers.

Rank.		Name.	Status.	Unit.	Date of Commission.	Present Rank.
Substantive and Acting.						
Major.Bvt/Lieut.Colonel.		G.B.O.Symons.D.S.O.	Reg.	C.R.E. 18th Division.	19. 10. 94.	19. 3. 17.
T/Lieut.A/Captain.		G.H.Kohl.	T.C.	Adjutant.	28. 8. 15.	14. 12. 17.
Captain.A/Major.		K.T.Gourlay. M.C.	Reg.	O.C. 79th Field Coy. R.E.	26. 7. 11.	10. 7. 18.
T/Lieut.A/Captain.		C.P.Geen. M.C.	T.C.	"	3. 6. 16.	26. 5. 18.
T/Lieutenant.		L.A.Mackay.	T.C.	"	6. 8. 15.	17. 11. 17.
T/2nd Lieutenant.		G.A.Young.	T.C.	"	1. 4. 17.	
T/2nd Lieutenant.		A.E.Haynes.	T.C.	"	1. 4. 17.	
T/2nd Lieutenant.		R.J.Reed.	T.C.	"	19. 8. 17.	
T/2nd Lieutenant.		P.E.Knight.	T.C.	"	17. 11. 17.	
T/Captain.A/Major.		G.Ledgard. M.C.	T.C.	O.C. 80th Field Coy. R.E.	25. 3. 15.	24. 3. 18.
T/Lieut.A/Captain.		R.Weir. M.C.	T.C.	"	7. 5. 16.	24. 3. 18.
T/Lieutenant.		A.J.Phillips.	T.C.	"	17. 11. 15.	1. 7. 17.
T/2nd Lieutenant.		S.Moare.	T.C.	"	28. 3. 17.	
T/2nd Lieutenant.		A.E.Watson.	T.C.	"	28. 10. 17.	
T/Captain.A/Major.		E.D.Alexander. M.C.	T.C.	O.C. 92nd Field Coy. R.E.	20. 3. 15.	7. 3. 18.
Lieut.A/Captain.		T.C.D.Davies.	T.R.	"	25. 2. 15.	14. 4. 16.
T/Lieutenant.		H.J.Parhom.	T.F.	"	9. 12. 14.	1. 6. 16.
T/2nd.Lieutenant.		B.Wood.	T.C.	"	15. 12. 17.	
T/2nd.Lieutenant.		R.D.Alexander.	T.C.	"	12. 1. 18.	
T/2nd.Lieutenant.		W.Hoyland.	T.F.	"	2. 6. 17.	
T/2nd.Lieutenant.		D.R.Thomas.	T.C.	"	2. 2. 18.	

P.T.O.

CASUALTIES AND CHANGES DURING THE MONTH OF AUGUST.

CASUALTIES.

T/2nd.Lieutenant.	A.C.James. R.E.	T.C.	80th Field Coy. R.E.	wounded in action	4/8/18.
2nd.Lieutenant.	H.D.Mackay. R.E.	Reg.	80th " " "	missing, believed prisoner of war.	6/8/18.
T/2nd.Lieutenant.	J.R.Bayley. R.E.	T.C.	92nd " " "	wounded in action	8/8/18.
T/2nd.Lieutenant.	A.F.Hall. R.E.	T.C.	92nd " " "	killed in action.	8/8/18.
T/2nd.Lieutenant.	F.J.Meen. R.E.	T.C.	92nd " " "	wounded in action.	8/8/18.
T/2nd.Lieutenant.	J.L.Davies. R.E.	T.C.	92nd " " "	Gassed.	22/8/18.
*T/2nd.Lieutenant.	J.R.Ogilvie. R.E.	TF.	80th " " "	wounded in action.	22/8/18.

*Since died of Wounds.

The undermentioned Officers joined the units as stated, from the R.E.Base Depot. 15th August 1918.

T/2nd.Lieutenant.	J.R.Ogilvie. R.E.T.F.	Joined	80th Field Coy. R.E.
T/2nd.Lieutenant.	J.L.Davies. R.E.T.C.	"	92nd. " " "
T/2nd.Lieutenant.	W.Hoyland. R.E.T.F.	"	92nd. " " "
T/2nd.Lieutenant.	D.R..Thomas. R.E.T.C.	"	92nd. " " "

****
* S E C R E T. *
****

Copy No..........

18TH DIVISION.

C.R.E.'s. OPERATION ORDER. NO. 136.

Reference Map.
BECOURT SHEET.
1/20.000.

Headquarters R.E.
18th Division.

20th August. 1918.

1. The 111 Corps will attack the enemy's position between BRAY and ALBERT at an hour, and on a date to be notified later.

2. The O.C. 80th Field Coy R.E. will place two Sections, and attached platoons at the disposal of 54th Infantry Brigade, for consolidation of Strong Points, and prepare the necessary dumps of wire etc.

The O.C. 92nd Field Coy R.E. will place two Sections, and attached platoons at the disposal of 55th Infantry Brigade, for consolidation of Strong Points, and prepare the necessary dumps of wire.

3. Os.C. 80th, and 92nd Field Coy's R.E. will arrange to construct portable footbridges for infantry to cross the river as may be required by B.Gs. of 54th, and 55th Infantry Brigades, and collect them under camouflage behind the Railway, or in some suitable place before ZERO.

4. BRIDGES.

O.C. 80th Field Coy R.E. will arrange to build 4 Weldon Trestle Bridges across the River ANCRE, as soon after ZERO as possible.

(a) About E.21.c.8.4.
(b) " E.21.d.1.7.
(c) " E.16.a.5.8.
(d) " E.10.a.8.0., or if there is no passable track fit for H.T. here, at about E.22.a.3.4.

O.C. 79th Field Coy R.E. will place his two trestles, and 60' of superstructure at the disposal of the 80th Field Coy R.E.

O.C. 92nd Field Coy R.E. will arrange to build 2 Weldon Trestle Bridges across the River ANCRE at about E.4.c.6.6. and W.28.b.9.4., as soon after ZERO as possible.

The above sites are suggested, and actual sites where bridges are made should be reported as soon as bridges are complete.

5. WELLS.

O.C. 80th Field Coy R.E. will send back, for testing, to nearest R.A.P., samples of water from any wells in BELLEVUE FARM, and mark the wells as directed by the R.A.M.C.

O.C. 92nd Field Coy R.E. will similarly deal with the wells at about E.4.b.5.1., and E.4.c.9.6., and report as to state of these wells, or any other well on the outskirts of ALBERT.

6. The 79th Field Coy R.E. will be in Divisional Reserve, and will be at the disposal of 53rd Infantry Brigade, should that Brigade be ordered forward as an Advanced Guard.

7. 180th Tunnelling Coy R.E. will be in Divisional Reserve, but parties will be told off ready to search for traps, and road mines, and to repair wells, when ordered by the Division.

8. PIONEERS.

O.C. 8th R. Sussex Regt. (Pioneers.) will detail one Company to make tracks, as shown on attached tracing, suitable for Horse Transport, as soon after ZERO as possible.

Timber for Plank roads is available, and 4 tip carts for brick.

9. Two Companies will be in Divisional Reserve, and be kept in readiness to reconnoitre, and repair, main traffic lines through ALBERT. and the ALBERT - La-BOISELLE - CONTALMAISON, and the ALBERT - BECORDEL Roads, as ordered.

10. Divisional Headquarters will be at CONTAY, each Field Company, 180th Tunnelling Company, and 8th R. Sussex Regt, should send one cyclist orderly to report to C.R.E. about 3 hours after ZERO.

11. Please acknowledge.

Issued at:- ....

[signature]
Captain R.E.
for, C.R.E. 18th Division.

Distribution:-

Copy No.	1.	O.C. 79th Field Coy R.E.
" "	2.	O.C. 80th Field Coy R.E.
" "	3.	O.C. 92nd Field Coy R.E.
" "	4.	O.C. 180th Tunnelling Coy R.E.
" "	5.	O.C. 8th R. Sussex Regt. (Pioneers.)
" "	6.	53rd Infantry Brigade.
" "	7.	54th Infantry Brigade.
" "	8.	55th Infantry Brigade.
" "	9.	"G" 18th Division.
" "	10.	"A/Q" 18th Division.
" "	11.	A.D.M.S. 18th Division.
" "	12.	C.E. 111 Corps.
" "	13.	War Diary.
" "	14.	Spare.

Headquarters 18th Divl. Engineers.

Appendix to War Diary for August.

Casualties in Field Companies. R.E.

OFFICERS............7.

O.Rs. .... 72.

Army Form C. 2118

WAR DIARY
or
INTELLIGENCE SUMMARY

(Erase heading not required.)

Instructions regarding War Diaries and Intelligence Summaries are contained in F.S. Regs., Part II. and the Staff Manual respectively. Title Pages will be prepared in manuscript.

WAR DIARY FOR SEPTEMBER 1918., H.Q., R.E. 18TH DIVISION.

Place	Date	Hour	Summary of Events and Information	Remarks and references to Appendices
MONTAUBAN.	1st	2nd.	Divisional Headquarters in CATERPILLAR VALLEY. Field Companies working on Roads, Tracks, and WATER SUPPLY.	
COMBLES.	3rd.		On capture of SAILLY-SAILLISEL and ST PIERRE VAAST WOOD, C.R.E. moved up to COMBLES, - considerable difficulty over the watering of horses was experienced in COMBLES, owing to the 38th, and 47th Divisions wishing to water there, and the two petrol pumps continually breaking down owing to debris in wells.	
"	4th.		Relieved by 12th Division, C.R.E.'s. H.Q. moved back to CATERPILLAR VALLEY.	
MONTAUBAN.	5th	15th.	Division in rest, and training, Monuments erected by Field Companies, in TRONES WOOD.	
"	16th.		Field Companies moved forward.	
LIERAMONT.	17th.		C.R.E.'s H.Q. Moved to LIERAMONT, and take over partly from 12th Division, and 74th Division.	
"	18th	22nd.	Dummy tanks erected before dawn by 92nd Field Coy R.E., Attack on RONSSOY, and LEMPIRE. Developing Water Supply ST-EMILIE, and reconnoitring for water in RONSSOY, and LEMPIRE, and consolidation and wiring a C.T. to DUNCAN POST, and DOLEFUL POST, and work on roads.	
"	23rd	24th.	Handing over to 102nd U.S. Engineers, 27th American Division.	
COMBLES.	25th	27th.	H.Q. to COMBLES. 79th Coy R.E. to MAUREPAS. 80th Coy R.E. to COMBLES. 92nd Coy. NURLU.	
LIERAMONT.	28th.		H.Q. to LIERAMONT. 3 Field Companies to West of EPEHY.	
"	29th	30th.	Companies standing by to bridge ST QUENTIN Canal at VENDHUILE, reconnaissance only possible Reports handed over, Road to VENDHUILE made good, Dug-outs searched for traps,	

A list of documents attached is on the reverse side.

WAR DIARY.

List of Documents attached to WAR DIARY for September 1918.
-*-*-*-*-*-*-*-*-*-*-

C.R.E.'s. OPERATION ORDER. No. 137. dated 15th September.
" " " 138. dated 24th September.
" " " 139. dated 27th September.

Nominal Roll of Officers for month of September 1918. Showing Casualties, and Changes.

[signature]
Lieut Colonel R.E.
Commanding Royal Engineer, 18th Division.

11th October 1918.

SECRET.

COPY No. 14

102

18th DIVISION.

C.R.E.'s. OPERATION ORDER. No. 13/7.

Ref. Maps.
Sheets
62.c.N.E. & 62.D.N.W.

Headquarters R.E.
18th Division.

15th Sept. 1918.

1. An attack on a wide front will be carried out on a date and at an hour to be notified later with a view to securing a position affording good observation over the HINDENBURG Line. The III Corps will attack with the 74th.Div. on the right, the 18th Division on the right centre, the 12th Division on the left centre and 1 Bde. of the 58th Division on the left.

2. The 54th Bde. with 7th Bn.West Kent Regt., and one section of Tanks attached, will capture and consolidate the 1st objective (Green Line) on the Divisional Front.
The 55th Bde with 10th Bn.Essex Regt. attached will capture and consolidate the 2nd objective (Red Line) on the Divisional Front, and exploit success to the line of exploitation (Blue line).

3. 2 Sections of the 80th Field Coy.R.E. will be at the disposal of 54th Bde. for consolidation of the Green Line.

    2. Sections of the 92nd Field Coy.R.E. will be at the disposal of the 55th Bde. for consolidation of Red Line.

4.
    (a) The O.C.80th Field Coy.R.E. will detail special parties to reconnoitre and develop the Water Supply and report on roads, dumps, traps, etc, in area up to N and S Grid Line between squares   F.10. and F.11. and F.16. and F.17.

    (b) The O.C.92nd Field Coy. will similarly reconnoitre and develop the Area East of the N and S Grid Line between squares F.10 and F.11 and F.16 and F.17.

    N.B. Certain Water Supply Stores, Windlasses , Buckets, Chain Pumps, etc, are available at the R.E.Dump D.18.a.
    in Fwd Area
    Information re Water Supply was sent to Field Companies under my No.73/33. dated 14th Sept.

5. The 79th Field Coy.R.E. will be in Divisional Reserve and be prepared to make crossings over Trenches/through Wire as may be asked for by C.R.A.

6. The 182nd Tunnelling Coy.R.E., as soon as the situation admits, will detail parties to search for traps in STE. EMILIE, RONSSOY, LEMPIRE and along the main roads.

7. The 8th Royal Sussex Pioneers will as soon as the situation admits, reconnoitre and open up the roads:-

    (a) VILLERS FAUCON - F.8.a.6.4. - LEMPIRE - LE TOMBOIS FARM.

    (b) and furnish report and if feasible open up the road E.24.b. 0.4. - RONSSOY - F.16.c.8.0. - GILLEMONT ROAD.

    (c) Any additional roads on the attached tracing.

8. C.R.E's Headquarters will be at D.12.d.9.5. after 4.P.M. on 16th September.

P.T.O.

Page. 2.

9. Field Companies, 182 Tunnelling Coy R.E. and 8th Royal Sussex Pioneers will each send a cyclist orderly to report and stay at C.R.E's H.Q. at 8.A.M. 17th and will bring rations with them for consumption on 18th. *who*

10. Please acknowledge.

Issued at... 8.30.P.M.

Geo H Kohl
Captain. R.E.
for, C.R.E. 18th Division.

Distribution:-

Copy No.	1.	O.C. 79th Field Coy. R.E.
" "	2.	O.C. 80th Field Coy. R.E.
" "	3.	O.C. 92nd Field Coy. R.E.
" "	4.	O.C. 182nd Tunnelling Coy. R.E.
" "	5.	C.O. 8th Royal Sussex Pioneers.
" "	6.	53rd Infantry Brigade.
" "	7.	54th Infantry Brigade.
" "	8.	55th Infantry Brigade.
" "	9.	"G" 18th Division.
" "	10.	A/Q 18th Division.
" "	11.	A.D.M.S. 18th Division.
" "	12.	C.E. III Corps.
" "	13.	War Diary.
" "	14.	Spare.

SECRET   C.R.E. 18th Div. No. 42/33.

O.C. 79th Field Coy. R.E.
O.C. 80th Field Coy. R.E.
O.C. 92nd Field Coy. R.E.

1. 18th Division dismounted personnel(less troops now in forward area and one Bn. 55th Inf Bde.) will move by bus and march route to-morrow, 16th Sept. in accordance with Table 'A' on reverse.

2. 1st Line Transport will move to-morrow, 16th Sept., under the orders of formation and unit Commanders to vicinity of MOISLAINS, to move off not later than 7.A.M.

3. There will be no movement forward, of LIERAMONT until dusk.

4. All troops on the march will, on the approach of hostile aircraft, halt on the side of the road. There will be no movement until the enemy aircraft have disappeared.
Distances on the march will be observed and strict march discipline observed in accordance with SS.724.

5. Map Locations of Coy. H.Q. and Transport Lines will be reported to C.R.E. immediately on arrival.

6. Please acknowledge.

15/9/18.   Captain. R.E.
                                              for, C.R.E. 18th Division.

P. T. O.

PROVISIONAL BUS ARRANGEMENTS TABLE 'A'

Date	Formation or Unit.	Approx numbers embussing.	Embussing point.	Time.	Debussing point.	Remarks.
Sept. 16th	53rd Bde.Group. 53rd Bde H.Q. 79th Fd.Coy.	150.} 110.}	S.30.c.0.8.	9-0.A.M.	NURLU.	Concentration areas. 53rd Inf Bde as arranged with Bde. 53rd Bde relieve.
do.	54th Bde.Group.&H.Q. 80th Fd.Coy.	50.	T.21.d.0.6.	10-15.A.M.	do.	AIZECOURT-LE-Ses area 54th Inf.Bde
do.	Div.H.Q.Group.	200.	S.28.c.8.5.	12.noon.	do	
do	56th Bde.Group.&H.Q. 92nd Fd.Coy.R.E.	80.	S.30.b.0.4.	4-0.P.M.	do	55th Inf. Bde. SAULCOURT area.

* S E C R E T. *

Copy No. 13

18TH DIVISION.

C.R.E.'s OPERATION ORDER. NO. 138.

Reference Maps.
62.C, and 57.C.
1/40,000.

Headquarters R.E.
18th Division.

25th September 1918.

1. The 18th Division will be relieved in the line, by the 27th Division U.S.A. on the night of the 24/25th September 1918.

2. The 79th, and 92nd Field Companies R.E. will hand over work, and billets, and give all assistance, and information possible, to A. and B. Companies, 1st Battn 102nd U.S. Engineers respectively.

3. On completion of relief on the 25th Instant, the 79th Field Coy R.E. will move to the MAUREPAS Area, with the 53rd Infantry Brigade group.

    The 92nd Field Coy R.E. will move to the NURLU Area, with the 54th Infantry Brigade Group.

    The 80th Field Coy R.E. (as at present) in COMBLES AREA, with the 55th Infantry Brigade Group.

    The 79th, and 92nd Field Coys, should withdraw forward Sections to their Horselines on handing over bivouacs to the U.S. Engineers.

4. Tents, and Trench Shelters will be retained, and taken to new areas.

5. Personnel Railhead will be PERONNE.

6. All transport must be on the move by 8.a.m.

7. Locations of H.Q. and Transport Lines of each Company should be forwarded to this Office as soon after completion of move as is possible.

8. C.R.E.'s H.Q. will move to COMBLES on the 25th Inst.

9. Administrative Instructions are attached, (for Field Companies only.)

10. Acknowledge.

Issued at 3.30 p.m.

CB O Symons
Lieut Colonel R.E.
C.R.E. 18th Division.

Distribution over.

Distribution.

Copy No.	1.	O.C. 79th Field Coy R.E.
" "	2.	O.C. 80th Field Coy R.E.
" "	3.	O.C. 92nd Field Coy R.E.
" "	4.	O.C. 1st Btn 102 U.S. Engrs.
" "	5.	53rd Infantry Brigade.
" "	6.	54th Infantry Brigade.
" "	7.	55th Infantry Brigade.
" "	8.	"G" 18th Division.
" "	9.	"A/Q" 18th Division.
" "	10.	S.S.O. and O.C. Div Train.
" "	11.	O.C. 18th Div Signals.
" "	12.	C.E. III Corps.
" "	13.	War Diary.
" "	14.	Office.
" "	15.	Spare.

```
*****************
* S E C R E T. *
*****************
```
Copy No. 16

18TH DIVISION.

C.R.E.'s OPERATION ORDER. NO. 139.

Reference Map Sheet
MONTBREHAIN.
1/20.000.

Headquarters R.E.
18th Division.

27th September 1918.

1. The 18th Division will mop up VENDHUILE, and make good the crossings over the ST-QUENTIN CANAL.

2. The Canal is reported to be dry generally, with a few puddles, but will almost surely have a muddy bottom.

3. Should all the bridges be destroyed, it is proposed to make a few crossings for Infantry, and then concentrate on the three main traffic bridges for Horse Transport.

   (a). About S.26.d.7.5.
   (b).   "   S.26.d.5.9.
   (c).   "   S.26.a.8.3.

   N.B. Nature of Bridges, and Crossings, will depend on reconnaissance of River, which should be made by small parties as soon as the situation admits.
   Air Photographs, and all information about the Canal at present available is being supplied separately.

4. There is a III Corps Bridging Dump being made at E.14.b.6.4. where material is being collected for various forms of bridges, i.e. - Trestle - Crib Pier - Girder - and also road slabs, (list attached.)

   The Field Companies will send their Bridging Equipment loaded on wagons, to the vicinity of this Dump, at ZERO - plus 5 hours, should the pontoon equipment not be required, it can be offloaded here, left with a guard, and the wagons reloaded as required.

   The wagons of the 12th Division Field Coys, will be at this dump, and loaded as follows:-

   3 with Weldon Trestle equipment complete.
   3 with road slabs, - 3 with sleepers.

   These stores and wagons can be used by any Field Coy, and will be sent up by C.R.E. when asked for.

   O.C. 80th Field Coy R.E. will detail a party to be at this dump, to do the necessary loading, and unloading.

5.   The 79th Field Coy R.E. will make the bridges (a) & (b), and any footbridges required in between, 3 if possible.

   The bridge (b) should be so sited as to allow an INGLIS, or Class "A" Bridge to be made, the road being diverted as required.

   The 283rd A.T. Coy R.E. will be making these bridges as soon as the situation permits, and 1 Field Coy R.E. of the 12th Division the corresponding bridge over the R.ESCAUT.

6.   The 80th Field Coy R.E. will detail one Section to form part of the Composite Force, under the 54th Infantry Brigade, that accompanies the 107th American Infantry Regt. A party vide 4 above.
   The remainder of the Company, will, when the situation admits, cross the Canal, make the necessary bridges across the R. ESCAUT, and assist as necessary on the 3 main traffic bridges across the Canal.

7.   The 92nd Field Coy R.E. will make the bridge (c) above, and footbridges S.26.a. & b.
   Detail a party to reconnoitre and develop wells, and water supply in VENDHUILE and PUTNEY.

8.   A small wireless signal party will accompany the 79th Field Coy R.E. and will be installed in VENDHUILE, messages should be sent by this means by all Coys to 18th Division, as to state of bridges, completion of bridges etc. A special code will be issued.

9.   The 12th Division have a dump of various R.E. Stores, and material, including water supplies, at D.11. central.

10.   Route for transport from Bridging dump, will be:-
   E.15.a.0.4. - E.10. - X.25.c.1.4. - LEMPIRE - TOMBOIS FARM.

11.   PIONEERS.

   The 8th Bn R. Sussex Regt. (Pioneers.) will as soon as the situation admits make good for Lorry Transport the TOMBOIS FARM Road from the Cross roads F.15.d.8.8. through F.11. to VENDHUILE and PUTNEY, and side roads in VENDHUILE as shown Yellow on attached map.

   Half a Tunnelling Company from the V Corps will assist in searching for, and clearing road mines.

   Foden lorries loaded with stone ready to go forward will be sent up by C.R.E. should they be required.

   40 wheelbarrows can be drawn from the bridge dump at E.14.b.5.4.

12.   Notice boards should be erected indicating roads to bridges, wells etc.

13.   C.R.E.'s Headquarters will open at LIERAMONT to-morrow the 28th Instant.

14.   Please acknowledge.

Issued at: 9/... — C B Symons
                      Lieut Colonel R.E.
                      C.R.E., 18th Division.

Distribution.

O.C.   Copy No. 1.   O.C. 79th Field Coy R.E.
  "   "   2.   O.C. 80th Field Coy R.E.
  "   "   3.   O.C. 92nd Field Coy R.E.
  "   "   4.   O.C. 8th R. Sussex Regt.
  "   "   5.   53rd Inf Bde.
  "   "   6.   54th Inf Bde.
  "   "   7.   55th Inf Bde.
  "   "   8.   "G" 18th Division.
  "   "   9.   "A/Q" 18th Division.
  "   "   10.   O.C. 18th Div Signals.
  "   "   11.   O.C. 18th Bn M.G.C.
  "   "   12.   O.C. ... T. Coy R.E.
  "   "   13.   C.R.E. 12th Division.
  "   "   14.   C.R.E. 38th Division.
  "   "   15.   C.E. III Corps.
  "   "   16.   War Diary.
  "   "   17.   Office.
  "   "   18.   Spare.

Field Company Commanders.
O.C. 9th R. Sussex Regt.

Reference C.R.E.'s Operation Order No. 189 attached. Para 4. Herewith List of material referred to.

In addition to Complete INGLIS Bridge - Class "A", and Pontoon Bridges, (it is not anticipated that the last will be required) the following material will be available at the Bridging Dump, at L.14.b. Sheet 62.C.

The equivalent in slabs or Mining Timber of 6000 Road Slabs, also dogs, spikes, and nails.

3000' 1" boarding.

About 600 F.R. of Baulks - about 7" x 7".

About 500 sleepers.

Sundry Ropes, Blocks, and Tackle.

150 Round Spars.

Cork rafts - Wire netting Mats for crossing on) For Infantry
mud - Floating rafts.   ) in file.

50 R.S.Js.

10 Foden lorries are standing by loaded with stone ready to go forward on demand - brick and probably a great deal of useful timber will almost certainly be found in VENDAMME.

Nominal Roll of Officers. — 13th Divisional Engineers.

Rank. Substantive and Acting.	Name.	D.S.O.	Status	Unit.	Date of. Commission.	Date of. Present Rank.
Major. Bvt/Lieut Colonel.	C.S.O. Symons.		Regt.	C.R.E. 13th Division.	19. 10. 04.	19. 3. 17.
Captain. A/Major.	R.I. Gourlay. M.C.		Reg	O.C. 79th Field Coy R.E.	29. 7. 11.	10. 7. 16.
T/Lieut. A/Captain.	G.P. Been. M.C.		T.C.	"	5. 8. 15.	24. 5. 18.
T/Lieutenant.	H.A. Mackay.		T.C.	"	5. 8. 15.	17. 11. 17.
T/2nd Lieutenant.	G.A. Young.		T.C.	"	1. 4. 17.	
T/2nd Lieutenant.	R.J. Reed.		T.F.	"	19. 8. 17.	
T/2nd Lieutenant.	P.W. Knight.		T.C.	"	17. 11. 17.	
T/Captain. A/Major.	O. Hedwart. M.C.		T.C.	O.C. 80th Field Coy R.E.	25. 7. 15.	24. 5. 18.
T/Lieut. A/Captain.	E. Weir. M.C.		T.C.	"	7. 5. 16.	24. 5. 18.
T/Lieutenant.	A.J. Phillips.		T.C.	"	17. 11. 16.	1. 7. 17.
T/2nd Lieutenant.	S. Hoare.		T.C.	"	28. 3. 17.	
T/2nd Lieutenant.	A.K. Watson.		T.C.	"	28. 10. 17.	
T/2nd Lieutenant.	H.R. Chambers.		T.C.	"	25. 3. 18.	
T/Lieut. A/Major.	T.C.S. Davies.		T.F.	O.C. 92nd Field Coy R.E.	25. 9. 12.	19. 9. 18.
T/Lieut. A/Captain.	H.J. Parison.		T.F.	"	9. 12. 14.	14. 9. 18.
T/Lieutenant.	H.E. Macdonald.		T.F.	"	2. 11. 16.	2. 5. 18.
T/2nd Lieutenant.	W. Hoyland.		T.F.	"	2. 6. 17.	
T/2nd Lieutenant.	S. Wood.		T.C.	"	15. 10. 17.	
T/2nd Lieutenant.	R.C. Alexander.		T.C.	"	12. 1. 18.	
T/2nd Lieutenant.	D.R. Thomas.		T.C.	"	9. 2. 18.	
T/2nd Lieutenant.	E. Crowther.		T.C.	"	23/2/18	

For Casualties, and Changes during the Month. — P.T.O.

CASUALTIES AND CHANGES DURING THE MONTH OF SEPTEMBER.

H.Q. R.E.

T/Lieut. A/Captain. G.H. Kohl. R.E. T.C. (Late Adjutant R.E.) Left to assume command of 69th Fd Co R.E. 28/9/19.

80th Field Coy R.E.

T/2nd Lieutenant. H.T. Chambers. R.E. T.C. Joined from R.E. Base Depot. 6th September.

79th Field Coy R.E.

T/2nd Lieutenant. A.R. Haynes. R.E. T.F. To Hospital Sick. 22nd September 19 18.

92nd Field Coy R.E.

T/Captain. A/Major E.D. Alexander. M.C.R.E. To Hospital Sick. 18th September. Evacuated to U.K.
T/2nd Lieutenant. E. Crowther. R.E. T.C. Joined from R.E. Base Depot. 6th September.
T/Lieutenant. H.E. Macdonald. R.E. T.F. Joined from R.E. Base Depot. 23rd September.

Commanding Royal Engineer, 19th Division.

1st October. 19 18.   Lieut Colonel R.E.

C.R.E. 18th Div No. R./221.

Headquarters.
18th Division.

    Herewith War Diary for H.Q. R.E. 18th Division, and Diaries for 79th. 80th. 92nd Field Coys R.E. for the month of October 1918.

10/11/18.
                            Lieutenant.
              for C.R.E. 18th Division.

Army Form C. 2118

WAR DIARY
or
INTELLIGENCE SUMMARY
(Erase heading not required.)

109

WAR DIARY FOR OCTOBER, 1918. H.Q., R.E. 18TH DIVISION.

Place	Date	Hour	Summary of Events and Information	Remarks and references to Appendices
LIERAMONT.	OCTOBER. 1st.		C.R.Es. Headquarters moved to BEAUCOURT. Field Companies moved on this and the following day to same area.	
BEAUCOURT.	2nd - 16th.		Division in rest. Field Companies carried out Training Programme. Lieut D.A. Mackay. R.E. T.C. (79th Field Coy R.E.) Joined H.Q. R.E. and took over the duties of Adjutant. (Date of appointment 28/9/18.) vice Captain G.H. Kohl. R.E. T.C. to 69th Field Coy R.E. on the 28/9/18. Lieut Mackay joined unit on the 8th from the R.E. Training School ROUEN.	
"	16th.		Transport of Field Companies commenced to move back to the Line.	
"	17th.		C.R.Es. H.Q. moved to RONSSOY WOOD. Field Companies proceeded by Train:- 79th to PREMONT. 80th to SERAIN.	
RONSSOY WOOD	18th.			
SERAIN.	19th.		C.R.Es. H.Q. moved to SERAIN. 92nd Field Coy R.E. to ELINCOURT. Division joined XIII Corps.	
MARETZ.	20th.		C.R.Es. H.Q. moved to MARETZ and took over from 66th Division.	
"	21st.		C.R.Es. Advanced H.Q. moved to REUMONT. All Field Coys moved to MAUROIS.	
"	22nd.		Preparations for the operations of the 23rd.	
"	23rd.		C.R.Es. H.Q. and all Field Coys R.E. moved to LE CATEAU. Field Coys worked on bridges over RICHEMONT Stream, and roads in newly occupied area.	
LE CATEAU.	24th.-31st.		Field Coys worked on roads, gas proofing cellars, wiring and water supplies in BOUSIES Area.	

Documents attached.

C.R.Es. Operation Instructions No. 1. Dated 20th October 1918.
Nominal Roll of Officers for the Month of October.

10th November 1918.

Lieutenant.
for, C.R.E. 18th Division.

```
***************
*  S E C R E T.  *
***************
```
Copy No. 14

18TH DIVISION ORDER No. 236.

C.R.E.'s. INSTRUCTIONS No. 1.

Ref maps. 57b.N.E. & 57b.S.E.
1/20.000.

Headquarters R.E.
18th Division.

20th October 1918.

1. At ZERO hour on "Z" day, the Third and Fourth Armies will attack. The Fourth Army is to form a defensive flank, facing Eastwards, to protect the major operation which will be carried out by the Third Army.

2. The attack of the XIII Corps will be carried out by the 25th Division on the right, and the 18th Division on the left; on the left of the 18th Division the 33rd Division of the V Corps will attack.

3. TASKS of BRIGADES.

    The 53rd Bde, on the right, and the 54th Bde on the left will capture the 1st, and 2nd Objectives on the front of the 18th Division. The 55th Bde will capture the 3rd objective. One Bn. 54th Bde will be held in Divisional Reserve.

4. (a) The 79th Field Coy R.E. will make the necessary reconnaissances of Roads. Water. R.E. Dumps. Dug-Outs. etc. in the right Brigade Sector.

    (b) The 80th Field Coy R.E. in the Left Brigade Sector.

    (c) The 92nd Field Coy R.E. will be in reserve, till the 55th Bde moves forward.

5. It is intended to have a Central Route for Runners. Wireless, and Cable. This will follow the central road from BONSIES to L.9.c.2.6.- thence to the Valley about L.14.central, thence down the Valley to RICHEMONT HILL.

    Notice boards, and pickets will be erected along this track by the 80th Field Coy R.E. up to L.14.central, and by the 79th Field Coy R.E. on from this point.

6. The 79th Field Company R.E. will be responsible for road crossings at the HALT. K.35.c.8.3. - GARDE MILL, and EVILLERS WOOD FARM.

    The 80th Field Coy R.E. from the Crossing at RICHEMONT MILL, and K.23.c.1.2., The level crossing at K.29.c.8.8. which should be made wide enough to take 4 or 5 lines of transport, before ZERO if possible.

P. T. O.
****

-2-

7. The 8th Bn. R. Sussex Regt. (Pioneers.) will clear the Roads:-

   (a) K.35.c.9.3. - EVILLERS WOOD FARM - CORBEAU. - TILEULS FARM - L.11.c.5.1.

   (b) K.35.a.1.5. - RICHEMONT MILL - K.18.d.3.0. - FOREST.

   (c) TILEULS FARM - FAYT FARM - EPINETTE FARM - LA BALANCE.

   (d) <u>ALTERNATIVE ROADS.</u>

   (i) L.1.d.4.8. - L.3.a.2.3. - BOUSIES-
   - or -
   (ii) L.7.a.4.7. - L.9.c.2.6. - BOUSIES.

8. C.R.E.'s Advanced H.Q. will open at REUMONT to-day. R.E. H.Q. Rear opens at MARETZ to-day.

9. Each Field Company, and Pioneers will send 1 runner to report to C.R.E. Advanced H.Q. at ZERO, plus 3 hours.

10. Field Companies R.E. and Pioneers to acknowledge.

Issued at:- 1350. Hours.

C B Symons

Lieut Colonel R.E.
C.R.E., 18th Division.

<u>Distribution.</u>

Copy No.	1.	O.C. 79th Field Coy R.E.
" "	2.	O.C. 80th Field Coy R.E.
" "	3.	O.C. 92nd Field Coy R.E.
" "	4.	O.C. 8th R. Sussex Regt. (Pioneers.)
" "	5.	53rd Inf Bde.
" "	6.	54th Inf Bde.
" "	7.	55th Inf Bde.
" "	8.	"G" 18th Division.
" "	9.	"A/Q" 18th Division.
" "	10.	O.C. 18th Bn M.G.C.
" "	11.	18th Div Arty.
" "	12.	18th Div Signals.
" "	13.	C.E. XIII Corps.
" "	14.	War Diary.
" "	15.	Office.

Nominal Roll of Officers. -- 18th Divisional Engineers.

Rank. Substantive. and Acting.	Name.	Status.	Unit.	Date of Commission.	Date of Present Rank.
Major. Bvt/Lieut Colonel.	C.B.O. Symons. D.S.O.	Reg.	C.R.E. 18th Division.	19. 10. 94.	19. 3. 17.
T/Lieut. A/Captain.	D.A. Mackay.	T.C.	Adjutant.	6. 6. 15.	28. 9. 18.
Captain. A/Major.	K.I. Gourlay. M.C.	Reg.	O.C. 79th Field Coy R.E.	26. 7. 11.	10. 7. 18.
T/Lieut. A/Captain.	G.P. Geen. M.C.	T.C.	"	3. 6. 16.	26. 5. 18.
T/Lieutenant.	H.E. MacDonald.	T.F.	"	1. 11. 16.	3. 5. 18.
T/Lieutenant.	G.A. Young.	T.F.	"	1. 4. 17.	1. 10. 18.
T/2nd Lieutenant.	R.J. Reed.	T.F.	"	19. 8. 17.	
T/2nd Lieutenant.	P.E. Knight.	T.C.	"	17. 11. 17.	
T/2nd Lieutenant.	E.F. Mackay.	T.C.	"	1. 6. 18.	
T/Captain. A/Major.	G. Ledgard. M.C.	T.C.	O.C. 80th Field Coy R.E.	25. 3. 15.	24. 3. 18.
T/Lieut. A/Captain.	R. Weir. M.C.	T.C.	"	7. 5. 16.	24. 3. 18.
T/Lieutenant.	A.J. Phillips.	T.C.	"	17. 11. 15.	1. 7. 17.
Lieutenant.	S. Hoare.	S.R.	"	28. 3. 17.	28. 9. 18.
T/2nd Lieutenant.	A.H. Watson. M.C.	T.C.	"	28. 10. 17.	
T/2nd Lieutenant.	H.T. Chambers.	T.C.	"	25. 2. 18.	
T/Lieut. A/Major.	T.C.B. Davies. M.C.	T.F.	O.C. 92nd Field Coy R.E.	25. 2. 15.	18. 9. 18.
T/Lieut. A/Captain.	H.J. Parham.	T.F.	"	9. 12. 14.	18. 9. 18.
T/2nd Lieutenant.	W. Hoyland.	T.F.	"	3. 6. 17.	
T/2nd Lieutenant.	B. Wood.	T.C.	"	15. 12. 17.	
T/2nd Lieutenant.	R.D. Alexander.	T.C.	"	12. 1. 18.	
T/2nd Lieutenant.	J.L. Davies. M.C.	T.C.	"	2. 2. 18.	

For Casualties, and Changes during the Month. — P.T.O.

CASUALTIES. AND CHANGES. DURING THE MONTH OF OCTOBER.

T/Lieut. A/Captain. D.A. Mackay. Joined H.Q. R.E., from 79th Field Coy R.E. and Assumed the duties of Adjutant, 18th Divisional Engineers, 28/9/18.

79th Field Coy R.E.

T/Lieutenant. H.E. MacDonald. Joined Unit from 92nd Field Coy R.E.   8. 10. 18.
T/2nd Lieut. E.F. Mackey. Joined Unit from R.E. Base Depot.   16. 10. 18.

92nd Field Coy R.E.

T/Lieutenant. H.E. MacDonald. Transferred to 79th Field Coy. R.E.   8. 10. 18.
T./2nd Lieut. J.L. Davies. Rejoined from Hospital.   7. 10. 18.
T/2nd Lieut. E. Crowther. Killed in Action.   25. 10. 18.
T/Lieut. A/Me.Jor. T.C.B. Davies. Wounded in Action. Remained at duty. 25. 10. 18.
T/2nd Lieut. D.R. Thomas. To Hospital Sick.   17. 10. 18.

1st November 1918.

                       Lieutenant.
                       for, C.R.E. 18th Division.

Army Form C. 2118

WAR DIARY
or
INTELLIGENCE SUMMARY
(Erase heading not required.)

Vol 38

Place	Date	Hour	Summary of Events and Information	Remarks and references to Appendices
			War Diary for November 1918. 18th Division H.Q. R.E.	
LE CATEAU.	1st – 3rd.		Headquarters R.E. were in LE CATEAU.	
"	4th.		C.R.E.'s Advanced Headquarters moved to EPINETTE FARM with 18th Division Battle H.Q. The attack on the MORMAL FOREST commenced on the morning of the 4th.	
"	6th.		C.R.E's. Rear Headquarters remained at LE CATEAU.	
"	6th.		C.R.E's Advanced H.Q. returned to LE CATEAU.	
"	6th – 13th.		C.R.E.'s. Headquarters were at LE CATEAU.	
NOYELLES	13th – 18th.		H.Q. R.E. moved to NOYELLES. Field Companies R.E. were engaged in the construction of Bridges over the R. SAMBRE. R. TARSY. and GRANDE HELPE.	
"	18th.		H.Q. R.E. moved from NOYELLES to MAUROIS.	
MAUROIS.	19th.		H.Q. R.E. moved back to SERAIN, and rejoined Divisional Headquarters.	
SERAIN.	19th – 30th.		At Serain. Companies engaged on the repair of Billets, in their respective Brigade Areas,	

ANNEXTURES.

C.R.E.'s Operation Instructions No. 1. of 1st November 1918.
C.R.E.'s Operation Instructions No. 2. of 3rd November 1918.
Nominal Roll of Officers. 18th Divisional Engineers, for month of November.

Pawlabay Captain R.E.
Adjutant 18th Divisional Engineers.

DISTRIBUTION.

Copy No.		Copy No.	
1.	79th Field Coy R.E.	10.	54th Inf Bde.
2.	80th Field Coy R.E.	11.	55th Inf Bde.
3.	92nd Field Coy R.E.	12.	18th M.G. Btn.
4.	8th R. Sussex Regt.	13.	18th Div Sigs.
5.	1 Sec. 182 T. Co. R.E.	14.	A.D.M.S. 18th Div.
6.	C.R.A. 18th Div.	15.	C.R.E. 38th Div.
7.	"G" 18th Div.	16.	C.R.E. 50th Div.
8.	"A/Q" 18th Div.	17.	C.E. XIII Corps.
9.	53rd Inf Bde.	18.	War Diary.
		19.	Office.

```
*****************
*   SECRET.     *                           Copy No........
*****************
```

18TH DIVISION.

C.R.E.'s. INSTRUCTIONS. NO: 1.

Ref Map Sheet.   Headquarters, R.E.
57.a.N.W.   18th Division.
1/20,000.

1st November 1918.

1. The Division will attack on "Z" Day, as outlined by C.R.E. to O.C. Field Companies R.E. and Pioneers.

2. **SECRECY.**

   The strictest secrecy is to be observed, only such as are immediately concerned with preparations for the attack being told of its intentions.

3. The following areas are allotted to the Field Companies, for Reconnaissance, and Development, as soon as the situation admits.

   79th Field Coy R.E.

   On the North. The Corps Boundary.
   On the South. RUISSEAU STREAM, and BRULÉS LANE. (incls)
   On the East.   PONT ROUTIER Road. (incls)

   80th Field Coy R.E.

   On the North. RUISSEAU Stream - BRULES LANE. (excls)
   On the South. The Divisional Boundary.
   On the East.   PONT ROUTIER Road. (incls.)

   92nd Field Coy R.E.

   The Area between North and South Divisional Boundaries, Eastwards of PONT ROUTIER ROAD.

   The usual reconnaissances, and early reports to C.R.E. should be made, of Roads, Bridges, Dumps of R.E. material, Tools, etc. and available sources of water supply, with pumps etc.
   Careful search should be made at all Cross roads, and Bridges, even when already damaged, for delay action mines, and Tank Traps.

4. The Field Companies will erect Notice Boards at the various Cross roads indicated by arrows on Map "C", and such other notices like Brigade H.Q., Battalion H.Q., etc, as Brigades may wish.

5. The Field Companies will detail parties to do the necessary repairs to the following roads in their Areas.

   BRULÉS LANE.
   CARIERE VIVIER LANE.
   CHEMIN-de-RAUCOURT.

```
                                              **********
                                                P.T.O.
                                              **********
```

- 2 -

6. **WATER.**

    The 80th Field Coy R.E. will make a Water Point in A.16.d. where a spring of good water is reported.

    The 92nd Field Coy R.E. will be prepared to erect 2-2300 gal tanks on the PREUX Road, about MARONNE Cross roads, if other sources of water are not found. - These will be filled by Lorry.

7. O.C. No. 1. Section. 182nd Tunnelling Coy R.E. will detail parties to search for Mines, and Traps, in the Roads, and in the cellars of HECQ and PREUX.

    His attention is particularly called to the main road from LANDRECIES to ENGLEFONTAINE, the Cross roads in the Villages and the Saw Mills in A.22.d. where large dug-outs are reported.

8. **EMPLOYMENT OF PIONEERS.**

    The following are the roads that will be opened for Lorry Transport if possible.

    (a) Main LE-QUESNOY - LANDRECIES Road.
    (b) ENGLEFONTAINE - HECQ - PREUX. Road.
    (c) ROBERSART - PREUX Road, to Cross Roads B.8.c.7.9.
    (d) Road from F.11.b.2.5. through the Village of HECQ, along HECQ Road to LA GUERRE Cross Roads.
    (e) Road from F.11.c.2.4. to PREUX A.20.d.5.6.
    (f) PONT ROUTIER Road.
    (g) FONTAINE Road.
    (h) Road from B.8.c.7.9. to L'ERMITAGE Cross Roads.

    Attention is called to the obstructions already placed by the enemy on some of these roads, as indicated by Photographs which have been supplied.

    One Platoon will accompany each of 83rd, and 84th Brigades R.F.A. to assist them in getting through, to take up their forward positions.

9. **SIGNAL COMMUNICATIONS.**

    Wireless, and Cable laying tanks, marked by blue & white flags, will follow the following route.

    (a) Cross Roads L.9.b.2.5.
    (b) Road Junction A.14.b.2.9.
    (c) Cross Roads A.21.d.4.8. and along PREUX Road, halting places will be at points (b) and (c) above, also at MARONNE Cross Roads, and at the RAUCOURT Road.

10. Field Companies, and Pioneers will send a runner to C.R.E.'s H.Q. the location of which will be sent later, at ZERO plus 2 hours.

11. **ACKNOWLEDGE.**

    Issued at....1800....hours.

    C B Symons
    Lieut Colonel R.E.
    C.R.E. 18th Division.

    For Distribution see attached -

```
****************
*  S E C R E T. *                                    Copy No..........
****************
```

18TH DIVISION.

C.R.E.'s. INSTRUCTIONS. NO. 2.

Ref. Map Sheet.   Headquarters. R.E.
57.a.N.W.   18th Division.
1/20.000.

3rd November 1918.

1. With reference to 18th Division Order No. 241. and 18th Division Instructions Nos 1. & 2., and C.R.E's. Instructions No. 1.

2. In the event of the 55th Brigade continuing the Advance beyond the GREEN LINE on "Z" plus 1 day to the Line of the R. SAMBRE., the 92nd Field Company R.E. will continue to make the reconnaissances in the Divisional Area, and erect sign boards on important cross-roads.

3. The 80th Field Company R.E. will be prepared to repair, or make, another Pontoon Bridge across the R. SAMBRE at O.14.b.3.7. and assist in the searching for TRAPS in SASSEGNIES.

   O.Cs. 79th. and 92nd Field Companies R.E., will place their bridging equipment at the disposal of O.C. 80th Field Coy R.E.

4. The 79th Field Coy R.E. will be in Reserve.

5. PIONEERS.

   The 8th Bn. The R. Sussex Regt. (Pioneers.) will make good the following roads:-

   (a) LANDRECIES Road from L'ERMITAGE Cross-roads to B.11.a.2.7.
   (b) PONT-du-BOIS Road to PETIT PARIS and SASSEGNIES.
   (c) PASSE-du-FEU Road to LA CARMAGNOLE and SASSEGNIES.

6. C.R.E.'s Advanced Headquarters will open at EPINETTE FARM at ZERO HOUR.

7. ACKNOWLEDGE.

Issued at:- 12.40. hours.

for
Lieut Colonel. R.E.
C.R.E., 18th Division.

Distribution as for. INSTRUCTIONS. NO. 1.

Nominal Roll of Officers. — 18th Divisional Engineers.

Rank. Substantive. and Acting.	Name.	Status.	Unit.	Date of Commission.	Date of Present Rank.
Major. Bvt/Lieut Colonel.	C.B.O. Symons. D.S.O.	Reg.	C.R.E. 18th Division.	19. 10. 94.	19. 3. 17.
T/Lieut. A/Captain.	D.A. Mackay.	T.C.	Adjutant.	6. 6. 15.	28. 9. 18.
Captain. A/Major.	K.I. Gourlay. M.C.	Reg.	O.C. 79th Field Coy R.E.	26. 7. 11.	10. 7. 18.
T/Lieut. A/Captain.	G.P. Geen. M.C.	T.C.	"	3. 6. 15.	26. 5. 18.
T/Lieutenant.	H.E. MacDonald.	T.F.	"	2. 11. 15.	5. 5. 18.
T/Lieutenant.	G.A. Young.	T.F.	"	1. 4. 17.	1. 10. 18.
T/2nd Lieutenant.	R.J. Reed.	T.F.	"	19. 8. 17.	
T/2nd Lieutenant.	P.E. Knight.	T.C.	"	17. 11. 17.	
T/2nd Lieutenant.	E.F. Mackey.	T.C.	"	1. 6. 18.	
T/Captain. A/Major.	G. Lodgard. M.C.	T.C.	O.C. 80th Field Coy R.E.	25. 5. 15.	24. 3. 18.
T/Lieut. A/Captain.	R. Weir. M.C.	T.C.	"	7. 5. 16.	24. 3. 18.
T/Lieutenant.	A.J. Phillips.	T.C.	"	17. 11. 15.	1. 7. 17.
Lieutenant.	S. Hoare.	T.C.	"	28. 5. 17.	28. 9. 18.
T/2nd Lieutenant.	A.H. Watson. M.C.	T.C.	"	28. 10. 17.	
T/2nd Lieutenant.	H.T. Chambers.	A.C.	"	23. 2. 18.	
T/Lieut. A/Major.	T.C.B. Davies. M.C.	T.F.	O.C. 92nd Field Coy R.E.	25. 2. 15.	18. 9. 18.
T/Lieut. A/Captain.	H.J. Parham.	T.F.	"	9. 12. 14.	18. 9. 18.
T/2nd Lieutenant.	W. Hoyland.	T.F.	"	2. 6. 17.	
T/2nd Lieutenant.	B. Wood.	T.C.	"	15. 12. 17.	
T/2nd Lieutenant.	R.D. Alexander.	T.C.	"	12. 1. 18.	
2nd Lieutenant.	R.A. Milne.	Reg.	"	25. 1. 18.	
2nd Lieutenant.	S.G. Galpin.	Reg.	"	25. 1. 18.	
T/2nd Lieutenant.	J.L. Davies. M.C.	T.C.	"	2. 2. 18.	

For Casualties, and Changes during the Month. P.T.O.

Casualties and Changes during the month.
-*-*-*-*-*-*-*-*-*-*-*-*-*-*-

Casualties :- Nil.

Changes. 2nd Lieut R.A. Milne. R.E. Joined 92nd Field Coy R.E. from R.E. Base Depot. 11/11/18.
          2nd Lieut S.G. Galpin. R.E. Joined 92nd Field Coy R.E. from R.E. Base Depot. 11/11/18.

30th November 1918.

                                    [signature]   Captain R.E.
                                         for, C.R.E. 18th Division.

Army Form C. 2118.

WAR DIARY
or
INTELLIGENCE SUMMARY
(Erase heading not required.)

AQ RE/18/D WD 39

Place	Date	Hour	Summary of Events and Information	Remarks and references to Appendices
			War Diary for December 1918. 18th Division. H.Q.,R.E..	
SERAIN.	1st -16th		At SERAIN, Companies engaged on repair of Billets, Destruction of "DUD" Shells, erection and repair of Baths, in their respective Brigade Areas.	
	17th.		C.R.E. Headquarters moved to LIGNY-EN-CAMBRESIS, Sheet.57.B.	
	17th -31st.		At LIGNY-EN-CAMBRESIS, Field Companies engaged as above.	

ANNEXURES.
****

Nominal Roll of Officers, 18th Divisional Engineers, for month of December.
****

D.A.Mackay
Captain.R.E.
Adjutant 18th Divisional Engineers.

117

NOMINAL ROLL OF OFFICERS. -- 18TH DIVISIONAL ENGINEERS.

Rank. Substantive and Acting.	Name.	Status.	Unit.	Date of Commission.	Date of Present Rank.
Major. Bvt/Lieut Colonel.	C.B.O. Symons. C.M.G. D.S.O.	Reg.	C.R.E. 18th Division.	19. 10. 94.	19. 3. 18.
T/Lieut. A/Captain.	D.A. Mackay.	T.C.	Adjutant.	6. 6. 15.	8. 10. 18.
Captain. A/Major.	K.I. Gourlay. M.C.	Reg.	O.C. 79th Field Coy R.E.	26. 7. 11.	10. 7. 18.
T/Lieutenant.	H.E. MacDonald.	T.F.	"	2. 11. 16.	3. 5. 18.
T/Lieutenant.	G.A. Young.	T.F.	"	1. 4. 17.	1. 10. 18.
T/2nd Lieutenant.	R.J. Reed.	T.F.	"	19. 8. 17.	
T/2nd Lieutenant.	P.E. Knight.	T.C.	"	17. 11. 17.	
T/2nd Lieutenant.	E.F. Mackey.	T.C.	"	1. 6. 18.	
T/Captain. A/Major.	G. Ledgard. M.C.	T.C.	O.C. 80th Field Coy R.E.	25. 3. 15.	24. 3. 18.
T/Lieut. A/Captain.	R. Weir. M.C.	T.C.	"	7. 5. 16.	24. 3. 18.
T/Lieutenant.	A.J. Phillips.	T.C.	"	17. 11. 15.	1. 7. 17.
Lieutenant.	S. Hoare.	S.R.	"	28. 3. 17.	28. 9. 18.
T/2nd Lieutenant.	A.H. Watson. M.C.	T.C.	"	28. 10. 17.	
T/2nd Lieutenant.	H.T. Chambers.	T.C.	"	23. 2. 18.	
T/Lieut. A/Major.	T.C.B. Davies. M.C.	T.F.	O.C. 92nd Field Coy R.E.	25. 2. 15.	18. 9. 18.
T/Lieut. A/Captain.	H.J. Parham.	T.F.	"	9. 12. 14.	18. 9. 18.
T/Lieutenant.	W. Heyland. ****	T.F.	"	2. 6. 17.	2. 12. 18.
T/2nd Lieutenant.	B. Wood.	T.C.	"	15. 12. 17.	
T/2nd Lieutenant.	R.D. Alexander.	T.C.	"	12. 1. 18.	
2nd Lieutenant.	R.A. Milne.	Reg.	"	25. 1. 18.	
2nd Lieutenant.	S.G. Galpin.	Reg.	"	25. 1. 18.	
T/2nd Lieutenant.	J.L. Davies. M.C.	T.C.	"	2. 2. 18.	
T/2nd Lieutenant.	R.A. Fitton.	T.C.	"	13. 7. 18.	

T/Lieutenant. W. Hoyland. is at present Sick in Hospital. Date of being evacuated. 1/12/18.

P. T. O.

CASUALTIES AND CHANGES DURING THE MONTH OF DECEMBER.

T/Lieut. A/Captain. G.P. Geen. M.C. R.E. (Late Second-in-Command) 79th Field Coy R.E. Accidently Injured 19th December 1918. Transferred to England. 14/12/18. Struck off the Strength. Authority 18th Div No. 67/417."A".

T/2nd Lieut. R.A. FITTON. R.E. T.C. Joined 92nd Field Coy R.E. From R.E. Base Depot. 17th December 1918.

1st January. 1919.

D.A.Mackay
Captain R.E.
Adjutant R.E., for C.R.E. 18th Division.

Army Form C. 2118

WAR DIARY
or
INTELLIGENCE SUMMARY
(Erase heading not required.)

Vol 4 0

119

Place	Date	Hour	Summary of Events and Information	Remarks and references to Appendices
LIGNY.	1st to 31st		War Diary for January 1919. Headquarters. 18th Divisional Engineers. -*-*-*-*-*-*-*- Headquarters R.E. at LIGNY with 18th Divisional H.Q. During the month the Field Companies, were engaged upon the work of Clearing their respective Brigade Areas of "Dud Shells, Grenades, and Bombs, and destroying them. Work has been done on Improvement of billets occupied by Troops, fitting of Recreation Rooms, etc. 9th February, 1919. C W Lynn Lieut Colonel R.E. Commanding Royal Engineer, 18th Division.	

Army Form C. 2118

WAR DIARY
or
INTELLIGENCE SUMMARY

(Erase heading not required.)

120

WAR DIARY FOR FEBRUARY, 1919.

Headquarters. 18th Divisional Engineers.

Headquarters R.E. 18th Division at LIGNY-en-CAMBRESIS with Divisional Headquarters.

Field Companies R.E. were engaged on the destruction of Dud Shells, Bombs, and Grenades during the month, and also work has been done in the repair of Bath Houses, Bridges, and Roads.

T/Lieut. A/Captain. D.A. MACKAY. R.E. T.C. left Headquarters R.E. to proceed to be demobilized on the 8th.

ANNEXTURES.

Nominal Roll of Officers. 18th Divisional Engineers, for the month of February, 1919.

9th March. 1919.

Lieut Colonel R.E.
Commanding Royal Engineer. 18th Division.

Place	Date	Hour	
LIGNY-EN-CAMBRESIS.(NORD.)	1st to 28th.		

NOMINAL ROLL OF OFFICERS. --- 18TH DIVISIONAL ENGINEERS.

Rank.		Name.	Status	Unit.	Date of.	
Substantive and	Acting.				Commission.	Present Rank
Major. Bvt/Lieut Colonel.		C.B.O. Symons. C.M.G. D.S.O.)	Reg.	C.R.E. 18th Division.	18. 10. 94.	19. 3. 17.
Captain.	A/Major.	K.I. Gourlay. M.C.	Reg.	O.C. 79th Field Coy R.E.	26. 7. 11.	10. 7. 18.
T/Lieutenant.		H.E. Macdonald.	T.F.	" " " " "	2. 11. 12.	8. 5. 18.
T/Lieutenant.		G.A. Young.	T.F.	" " " " "	1. 4. 17.	1. 10. 18.
T/Lieutenant.		R.J. Reed.	T.F.	" " " " "	19. 9. 17.	19. 2. 19.
T/Captain.	A/Major.	G. Ledgard. M.C.	T.C.	O.C. 80th Field Coy R.E.	25. 3. 15.	24. 3. 18.
T/Lieutenant.		A.J. Phillips.	T.C.	" " " " "	17. 11. 15.	1. 7. 17.
Lieutenant.		S. Hoare.	S.R.	" " " " "	29. 3. 17.	28. 9. 18.
T/Lieut.	A/Major.	T.C.B. Davies. M.C.	T.F.	O.C. 92nd Field Coy R.E.	25. 8. 15.	18. 9. 18.
T/2nd Lieutenant.		B. Wood.	T.C.	" " " " "	19. 12. 17.	
2nd Lieutenant.		S.O. Galpin.	Reg.	" " " " "	28. 1. 18.	
T/2nd Lieutenant.		J.L. Davies. M.C.	T.C.	" " " " "	2. 7. 18.	
T/2nd Lieutenant.		R.A. Fitton.	T.C.	" " " " "	1. 7. 18.	

For Casualties and Changes during the month, F.T.C.

CASUALTIES AND CHANGES DURING FEBRUARY. 1919.

H.Q. R.E.

T/Lieut. A/Captain. D.A. Mackey. R.E. T.C. Adjutant 18th Divisional Engineers, left Unit for demobilization on the 6th February. 1919.

79th Field Company R.E.

T/2nd Lieut. E.F. Mackey. R.E. T.C. Left Unit to proceed to the D.A.D.G.R. & E.. GRAVES CONCENTRATION at BEAULTE for duty, on the 28th February. Authority 18th Division wire No. A./152. of the 27th February.

80th Field Company R.E.

T/Lieut. A/Captain. R. Weir. M.C. R.E. T.C. Left Unit to be demobilized, on the 18th February.

T/2nd Lieutenant. A.H. Watson. M.C. R.E. T.C. Left Unit to be demobilized, on the 22nd February.

92nd Field Company R.E.

T/Lieut. A/Captain. H.J. Parham. R.E. T.F. Left Unit to be demobilized, on the 5th February. 1919.

28th February. 1919.

Lieut. Colonel R.E.
Commanding Royal Engineer. 18th Division.

C.R.E. 18th Div No. 22/92.

18th Division. 'A'.

Herewith War Diaries for the Month of March. 1919. for H.Q. R.E. 18th Division. 79th. 80th. and 92nd Field Companies R.E.

12th April. 1919.

Redgard.
Major. R.E.
A/C.R.E. 18th Division.

Army Form C. 2118

WAR DIARY
or
INTELLIGENCE SUMMARY
(Erase heading not required.)

HQRE 18D

No. 51 4 2

123

Place	Date	Hour	Summary of Events and Information	Remarks and references to Appendices
LIGNY-en-CAMBRESIS. (Nord.)	1st to 31st.		Headquarters. 18th Divisional Engineers. WAR DIARY FOR MARCH. 1919. Headquarters R.E. 18th Division at LIGNY-en-CAMBRESIS with Divisional Headquarters. Field Companies R.E. were engaged on the Construction of the XIII Corps I.C.S. (Ordnance) at CAUDRY., also work done on the repair of billets occupied by them at CAUDRY. ANNEXTURES. Nominal Roll of Officers, 18th Divisional Engineers for the month of March. 1919. 11th April. 1919. Edgar Major. R.E. A/C.R.E. 18th Division.	

NOMINAL ROLL OF OFFICERS. --- 18TH DIVISIONAL ENGINEERS.

Rank. Substantive and Acting.	Name.	Status.	Unit.	Date of Commission.	Present Rank.
Major. Bvt/Lieut Colonel. A/Lieut. Colonel.	C.B.O. Symons. C.M.G. D.S.O.	Reg.	C.R.E. 18th Division.	16. 10. 94.	19. 3. 17.
T/Lieut. A/Captain. T/2nd Lieutenant.	H.E. MacDonald. ※ (SEE BELOW) J.L. Davies. M.C. (ATTACHED TO COMPLETE CADRE. FROM 92ND COY. R.E.)	T.F. T.C.	O.C. 79th Field Coy R.E. "	3. 11. 16. 2. 2. 18.	3. 5. 18. 2. 2. 18.
T/Capt. A/Major. T/2nd Lieutenant.	H. Ledgard. M.C. R.A. Fitton. (ATTACHED TO COMPLETE CADRE FROM 92ND COY. R.E.)	T.C. T.C.	O.C. 80th Field Coy R.E. "	25. 3. 15. 13. 7. 18.	24. 3. 18. "
T/Lieut. A/Captain. T/2nd Lieutenant. T/2nd Lieutenant.	A.J. Phillips. B. Wood. R.D. Alexander. (Detached.)	T/Cam???? T.C. T.C. T.C.	O.C. 92nd Field Coy R.E. " " "	17. 11. 15. 13. 12. 17. 12. 1. 18.	1. 7. 17. " "
2nd Lieutenant.	S.G. Galpin.	Reg.	"	25. 1. 18.	

※ T/LIEUT. A/CAPT, H.E. MACDONALD. UNDER ORDERS TO PROCEED TO Nº 8 DEFENCE SUB SECTOR. FOR DUTY. IN THE CROSSING UP. ARMY.

For Casualties and Changes during the Month. P.T.O.

Casualties and changes during the Month of March, 1919.

79th Field Company R.E.

Capt. A/Major. K.I. GOURLAY. M.C. R.E. (Reg) Transferred to Command 208th Field Company. (Army of Occupation.) Authority Third Army. A/A.2481. 27/3/19. Left Unit. 13/3/19.

T/Lieutenant. G.A. Young. R.E. (T.F.) Left Unit to be demobilized on the 16th March. 1919.
T/Lieutenant. R.J. Reed. R.E. (T.F.) Left Unit to be demobilized on the 16th March. 1919.

80th Field Company R.E.

T/Lieutenant. A.J. Phillips. R.E. (T.C.) Transferred to Command 92nd Field Company R.E. on 7th March. 1919. Authority for transfer. 18th Div No. 19/568. A. of 9/3/19.

Lieutenant. S. Hoare. R.E. (S.R.) Transferred to IXth Corps H.Q. (2nd Army.) Army of Occupation, Left 22/3/19. Authority for transfer A.G's. No. A.G. 10336.IX.(O) of 13/3/19.

92nd Field Company R.E.

T/Lieut. A/Major. T.C.B. Davies. M.C. R.E. (T.F.) Left Unit to be demobilized on the 8th March. 1919.
T/2nd Lieut. J.L. Davies. M.C.R.E. (T.C.) *Attached* to 80th Field Coy R.E. to complete Cadre.
T/2nd Lieut. R.A. Fitton. R.E. (T.C.) *Attached* to 80th Field Coy R.E. to complete Cadre.

28th March. 1919.

Major. R.E.
for.Lieut Colonel R.E.
Commanding Royal Engineer. 18th Division.

C.R.E. 18th Div No. 22/93.

Headquarters.
18th Division Packet.

Herewith War Diaries, for the month of April, of H.Q., R.E. 18th Division. 79th. 80th. and 92nd Field Companies R.E.

Lieut Colonel.R.E.
12th April. 1919.   C.R.E. 18th Div Packet.

Army Form C. 2118

WAR DIARY
or
INTELLIGENCE SUMMARY

(Erase heading not required.)

Instructions regarding War Diaries and Intelligence Summaries are contained in F. S. Regs., Part II. and the Staff Manual respectively. Title Pages will be prepared in manuscript.

Place	Date	Hour	Summary of Events and Information	Remarks and references to Appendices
LIGNY-en-CAMBRESIS. (Nord.)	1st to 31st.		Headquarters. 18th Divisional Engineers. —*—*—*—*—*—*—*—*—*—*—*—*— WAR DIARY FOR APRIL. 1919. Headquarters R.E. 18th Division at LIGNY-en-CAMBRESIS. (Nord.) with Divisional H.Q. Field Companies R.E. employed on checking, and cleaning transport and equipment, and packing same. 11th May. 1919. [signature] Lieut Colonel R.E. C.R.E. 18th Division Packet.	

www.ingramcontent.com/pod-product-compliance
Lightning Source LLC
Chambersburg PA
CBHW081422160426
43193CB00013B/2170